COMMEMO
PLAQUᴇꜱ
OF
CHELTENHAM

CELEBRATING
PEOPLE, PLACES
AND EVENTS

by *PETER SMITH*
and
SUE ROWBOTHAM
with maps
by Brian White

Published by
REARDON PUBLISHING
PO Box 919, Cheltenham, Glos, GL50 9AN.
Website: www.reardon.co.uk
Email: Reardon@bigfoot.com
Tel: 01242 231800

Copyright © 2009
Reardon Publishing

Written and Compiled
by
Peter Smith & Sue Rowbotham

Layout and Design
by
Sue Rowbotham

ISBN 1 873877 93 5
ISBN (13) 9781873877937

Printed Through
World Print Ltd

A PERSONAL DEDICATION

PETER SMITH (1916 - 2007)

1 - Peter and Judy Smith celebrate their 60th wedding anniversary in 2006

I would like to dedicate this book to Peter Smith, a quiet, unassuming but determined driving force, who worked tirelessly to promote and to celebrate his adopted town of Cheltenham, its history and its people.

Peter and his ever-supportive wife Judy moved to Cheltenham in 1962 and soon established themselves. Peter was often to be seen about the town, instantly recognisable by his shock of thick white hair and his purposeful stride. His interests were many and varied, and he inspired us all with his enthusiasm, his dedication, his boyish sense of humour and most of all with his energy.

Peter and Judy played an active part in the activities of many groups. Peter joined Cheltenham Civic Society in 1971. He was a founder member of the Lansdown Probus Club and of Leckhampton Local History Society, and often carried out Church Watch duties at St Mary's Parish Church. He was regularly to be seen collecting funds for Cheltenham Samaritans and the Royal National Lifeboat Institution, standing on what became known as 'Peter's spot' on Boots' Corner.

Both Peter and Judy Smith joined the Cheltenham Local History Society at the Society's second meeting in 1982, and were regular attendees after that date. Peter served on the Local History Society Committee for eight years, including five as Publicity Officer. In 1989 he became a founder member of the Society team who indexed the *Cheltenham Examiner newspaper* (1839-1913). He led the team for many years and saw the project to its successful completion in 2006, providing an invaluable resource for anyone with an interest in the history of Cheltenham. The index is searchable online at the Local History Society's website: www.cheltlocalhist.btik.com.

Peter is, perhaps, best remembered as Plaque Officer for the Cheltenham Civic Society, coordinating the Society's commemorative plaques scheme from 1995-2005. He also lovingly recorded details of the many other commemorative plaques, large and small, old and new, erected by individuals or groups in the town. In 2001 he was given the Alderman Charles Foster MBE award in well-deserved recognition for his voluntary work in Gloucestershire and, in particular, for his untiring efforts for the Cheltenham Civic Society.

Peter initially approached me with a thick bundle of closely-spaced, hand-typed pages on Cheltenham's commemorative plaques for inclusion in the *Cheltenham Local History Society Journal*. As Editor I concluded that the article required more space than was available in the *Journal* so we agreed that it should be published as a separate booklet. I sourced illustrations from across the world and commissioned maps from ex-Dowty draughtsman Brian White. The booklet grew into the substantial book that you see here over a period of several years, as a result of my own additional research, further information from Peter's meticulous records, and thanks to many other people and sources. To my profoundest regret Peter did not live to see the publication of this book. Thank you for your dedication and your vision Peter. I hope you approve.

Sue Rowbotham

FOREWORD

This publication is a record of the blue and green commemorative plaques unveiled by Cheltenham Civic Society since 1982, and the stories behind each plaque. It also includes earlier plaques fixed by other bodies, such as the Cheltenham Public Libraries Committee, commemorating notable persons who have lived in the town.

There are obviously many other commemorative plaques on and in public buildings, colleges, schools, hospitals and homes in Cheltenham, all of which have a story to tell. For example the town's leisure centre, Leisure@Cheltenham, was severely damaged when the building was inundated by millions of gallons of muddy water from nearby Pittville Lake during the disastrous floods that struck Gloucestershire in July 2007. A plaque was unveiled at the official reopening of the centre on 27 September 2008, following a £5m refurbishment programme. The plaque marks the deepest point that the flood water reached in the building (1.2m).

Of course there are also many plaques on park benches, at the bases of trees and elsewhere remembering individual loved ones, including a brass plaque in memory of my co-author, Peter Smith, which is located on a bench facing the bandstand in Montpellier Gardens, one of his favourite locations in Cheltenham. Unfortunately there are too many of these other plaques to be included here, but take time to stop and read the dedications if you can spare a moment. They all form part of the history of our town.

Inevitably this publication will be incomplete as further plaques are unveiled by the Civic Society in years to come. For a list of all current Society plaques and their locations go to the Society web site at www.cheltenhamcivicsociety.org.uk.

We hope that you will enjoy walking around Cheltenham locating the commemorative plaques described here, and that you will learn a little more about the people, places and events that they celebrate, and the stories behind them.

2 - Parmoor House, home of Cheltenham Civic Society since 1964

CHELTENHAM CIVIC SOCIETY

The first Cheltenham Civic Society was formally inaugurated in 1925 with objectives very similar to those of the modern Society, but by the end of the 1930s the Council (Committee) was only meeting once a year. In September 1950 a 'Regency Society' was formed with the intention of joining forces with the remaining members of the Civic Society and the Cheltenham branch of the Georgian Group but by the end of the 1950s that had also become moribund.

In the mid 1950s an ex-fighter pilot, Ian Nairn, wrote a strong article in the *Architectural Review* making people aware of the spread of 'Subtopia' - the spoiling of towns by poor design, traffic, wires, signs, and other street clutter - everything that was ruining their appearance. He led a crusade touring the country and gave a lecture to a packed audience in the then Cheltenham Art Gallery. As a result a new Cheltenham Civic and Rural Society was born in 1958 and nationally the Civic Trust was formed, chaired by Duncan Sandys, and with which the Society was registered. The Regency Society was amalgamated with the Civic and Rural Society in 1962 to become The Cheltenham Society ('Civic' was added later). At about this time the Society raised strong sustained objections at Public Enquiries to the County Council's plans for Cheltenham - the main objection was one of principle: that there should be traffic and pedestrian segregation (which took another 30 years to achieve). Later motorway-style road schemes crossing the town, proposed by the planning authorities and an outside consultant, were also opposed.

The Objects in the Civic Society Constitution are wide-ranging, but the core activity has always been commenting on planning applications (though in the early years they were confidential to the applicant) and responding to development plans. The Society is an official consultee in the Local Plan. However the Society is not a negative body. For example, it has promoted the 'Chelt Walk' with ongoing maintenance and planting; and has also cleared an old graveyard of mountains of rubbish and trees to create a quiet area. This is now known as Jenner Gardens, and the Society is represented on a committee to fully restore it. The Society has always been concerned about the town's trees, parks and gardens. In 1994 it raised £22,000 and restored the bandstand in Montpellier

Gardens - at that time in a gross state of dereliction - and staged its first concert, all within seven months!

Civic Society member Roger Beacham formed a committee in the 1960s and 1970s which compiled a list of proposed commemorative plaques, but nothing further was done, mainly due to cost. It was not until 1982 when the Handley Page Society approached the Civic Society suggesting a plaque for Handley Page's birthplace that the idea of sharing costs was mooted. The Society has been erecting plaques ever since to mark people, sites or events of national or local renown - round blue ones for people and rectangular green ones for locations or events. Every plaque has the co-sponsor recorded on it - an organisation connected with the person or site. The co-sponsor is always represented at the unveiling ceremony.

For many years the Society has also run the annual Civic Award scheme which is funded by the Borough Council. Awards and Commendations by an independent judging panel are given in four categories: for the design of a new building, for the restoration of a building, for an improvement to the built environment and for a new or restored shop front. You may spot Civic Award plaques on buildings in the town.

3 - Civic Award on Summerfield House

In 1964 Lord Parmoor gave us his house - 13 Lypiatt Terrace - '*that the Society should have a headquarters from which it can pursue its activities and use every endeavour to influence the future development of the Town so that it's character may, as far as possible, be preserved, and its beauty enhanced*'. The availability of Parmoor House, as it became named, has played a valuable part in the life of the Society. Society members enjoy a stimulating programme of related lectures throughout the year and take part in open forums, visits and social events. Rooms at Parmoor House are available for hire and are the venue for a number of local societies' and groups' activities.

Phil Newcombe, Vice-President, Cheltenham Civic Society

ACKNOWLEDGEMENTS

I would like to thank Chairman John Henry and the members of Cheltenham Civic Society Executive Committee for waiting so patiently as this work evolved from a hand-typed article to its completed form. In particular I would like to thank Phil Newcombe, for his careful review of the facts, and Christine Tustin for liaising with the Committee throughout the project and for her judicious proof-reading.

My special thanks go to Brian White, who used his masterly skills as both a draughtsman and calligrapher to produce the essential maps. My thanks must also go to Jill Waller for lending me her encyclopaedic knowledge and comprehensive archive of Cheltenham history, and for her trusty proof-reading skills. Also thanks to Nick Reardon of Reardon Publishing, for his advice and guidance on the process of publication, and to Geoff and Elaine North for allowing me to dip into their extensive archive of images of Cheltenham.

I gratefully acknowledge the work of Roger Beacham and members of the original Cheltenham Society's Commemorative Plaques Sub-Committee whose research into the early plaques proved invaluable. Thanks also to Helen Brown and Dr Steven Blake at Cheltenham Art Gallery and Museum, and to the staff at Cheltenham Local and Family History Library. I would also like to thank the *Gloucestershire Echo* for reporting many of the plaque unveiling ceremonies since 1982, and for providing the Civic Society with an excellent photographic record of these events.

Thanks to John Adams in Melbourne, and Sean Fagan in Kellyville, near Sydney, New South Wales who generously shared their enthusiasm for poet Adam Lindsay Gordon and the history of rugby league respectively from the other side of the world.

Finally, and most of all, I would like to thank my husband Steve, my children James and Emma, and all my friends for supporting me through this project. I could not have done it without you.

My thanks to the following for allowing me to reproduce these images:

Helen Brown (Cheltenham Art Gallery & Museum), 10, 41, 55, 90, 117;
Jill Barlow (Cheltenham College Archives), 12;
Cheltenham Civic Society, 15, 21, 47, 54, 85;
Stephen Clarke, 2, 91;
Sean Fagan (RL1908.com), 99;
Scott Givens (Taxus Buccata Books), 66;
Dave Martin, 52;
Carolyn Mills, Roy Trotter (Cheltenham Cricket Club), 68;
Geoff & Elaine North, 1, 67, 71, 88, 95, 102-3, 105;
David Reed (Soldiers of Gloucestershire Museum), 87;
David Reynolds (Brian Jones Fan Club, Cheltenham), 29;
Russell Self, 46;
Mike Smith (Gloucestershire Media), 9, 50, 60, 61, 62, 106-8, 128-9;
Jill Waller, 32, 42, 65, 69, 72, 75, 93, 101, 118;
Martin & Andrea Warburton, 79-80;
John Whittaker, 31;
Chris Wilson (Glos. Warriors RLFC), 98.

The following illustrations were taken from the on-line encyclopaedia Wikipedia (en.wikipedia.org), and are defined as being 'in the public domain': 4, 5, 22, 24, 25, 27, 48, 57, 78, 84, 116, 126, 127.

The remaining photographs and other images were taken from my own collection.

Every attempt has been made to establish and acknowledge all illustration copyright owners. I apologise if any have been omitted or are incorrect.

Sue Rowbotham

CIVIC SOCIETY
BLUE PLAQUES

PEOPLE

SIR BENJAMIN BAKER (1840-1907)
Civil Engineer
4 Cambray Place (map 2 no.8)

In summer a flowering creeper on 4 Cambray Place (now Tailor's) obscures the blue plaque which commemorates Sir Benjamin Baker, one of Britain's greatest civil engineers. Pulling the creeper aside will reveal that he lived as a young man in Farm Cottage which had existed on the site prior to the present building.

Born near Frome in Somerset in 1840 Benjamin Baker was educated at Cheltenham Grammar School. He served an apprenticeship at Neath Ironworks, South Wales before joining the engineering offices of Sir John Fowler as an assistant engineer. By 1875 he had become Fowler's partner.

4 - Sir Benjamin Baker

5 - Forth Bridge

Benjamin Baker's greatest achievement was as chief designer of the Forth Bridge in Scotland. The bridge, started in February 1883, completed the east coast railway route between London and Aberdeen. It spanned the Firth of Forth, connecting the city of Edinburgh with Fife. The 1½ mile bridge, constructed of almost 54,000 tons of steel, was the biggest in the world when it was completed in 1891. Today it is the world's oldest cantilever bridge, and is still very much in use.

This great engineer also played a leading role in the construction of London's first railways and one of the capital's first underground lines, originally called the Baker Street and Waterloo line, later renamed the Bakerloo line. Among many other projects Baker designed the cylindrical vessel that brought Cleopatra's Needle to London from Egypt (1877-8), and was consulting engineer for the Hudson River Tunnel, New York (1888-91). He received a knighthood in 1902 for his design for the first Aswan dam across the Nile (1899-1902).

Benjamin Baker was a member of the Royal Society and President of the Institute of Civil Engineers from 1895-6. In 1934 the Institute inaugurated the Baker Medal, still awarded annually, for services to development of, or investigation into bridges, dams, tunnels, soil mechanics, foundations, transport, research and materials.

Baker died in Pangbourne, Berkshire on 19 May 1907 and is buried in Idbury, near Chipping Campden, Gloucestershire. In 1922 Cheltenham Grammar School acknowledged him as one of its most successful pupils, by naming one of its six school houses after him. The house name remained in use until 1971.

The blue commemorative plaque to Sir Benjamin Baker was unveiled on 19 January 1985 by Mr A.D. Reeve, Senior Vice-President of the Institute of Civil Engineers, which had co-sponsored the plaque. The *Gloucestershire Echo* published a photograph of the ceremony with the Mayor, Councillor Gerry Bingham, David Phillips, Chairman of the Civic Society (1979-89) and others attending.

6 - 4 Cambray Place

JOSEPHINE BUTLER (1828-1906)
Social Reformer
Wellington Mansions, London Road (map 4 no.22)

7 - Josephine Butler, 1851

The great Victorian social reformer Josephine Elizabeth Butler (née Grey) moved to Cheltenham in 1857 when her husband Rev. George Butler was appointed Vice-Principal of Cheltenham College. The move may have been prompted by George's liberal ideas, which had conflicted with those widely held at Oxford where he had been an examiner of schools. The Butlers lived at The Priory, a fine Regency house on the corner of London Road and Priory Street. George and Josephine shared similar political views and during the American Civil War (1861-5) they encountered a great deal of hostility in Cheltenham when they expressed their support for the anti-slavery movement. Josephine's independent views on Irish Home Rule, the Boer War, women's suffrage and other issues found public expression through her many books, pamphlets, periodical contributions and letters to the Press.

The couple's fourth child and only daughter Eva, aged six, died in 1863 after falling down the stairs at The Priory, and the family's grief following this tragic accident may well have prompted George to accept an invitation to become Principal of Liverpool College. The family moved to Liverpool in January 1866 and Josephine, still dealing with the pain of her loss, described her state of mind at that time: *'I became possessed with an irresistible desire to go forth and... meet with people more unhappy than myself... and to say... "I understand. I, too, have suffered... It was not difficult to find misery in Liverpool."'*

The Butlers' house in Liverpool became a home for women needing assistance, who had been rescued from the streets and workhouses. The family later raised funds for a house near their own as a House of Rest (subsequently known as the Home for Female Incurables).

In 1869 Elizabeth Wolstenholme asked Josephine to lead the campaign against the Contagious Diseases Acts of 1866. After much deliberation, she accepted and her husband remained at home with the children and supported her in his lectures. There is a stained glass window in Liverpool's Anglican Cathedral dedicated to Josephine Butler.

It would be wrong to imagine Josephine Butler as a severe woman. According to her great-niece Beverley Grey '...*she was uncommonly beautiful, with gorgeous hair, dressed in the height of fashion, spoke and read several languages, could paint and play the piano to professional standards, and had a ringing sense of humour*'.

The Priory was demolished in 1968 and was replaced by an office block known as Mercian House. On 23 July 1983 Jack Nutley, Josephine Butler Society Chairman, unveiled a blue Civic Society plaque (see p.13) on the building in the presence of the Mayor, Councillor Roy Merchant. Fifteen years later Mercian House was demolished. Rev. Dr Richard Cleaves and his wife from nearby Highbury Church, keen advocates of Josephine's work, feared that the plaque would be lost and expressed their concern to the Josephine Butler Society. Fortunately the plaque was saved by Robert Wilson, then Civic Society Chairman.

8 - Wellington Mansions, site of The Priory

In 1999 Countryside Properties erected Wellington Mansions on the Priory site; the architecture echoing that of the original building. On 15 October 1999 Highbury Church staged a play on Josephine's life performed by Anna Briggs. The following day the original plaque, generously refurbished by the developers, was unveiled on Wellington Mansions by Valerie Gore, Josephine Butler Society Chairman. Also present were Beverley Grey; Mayor Councillor David Banyard; Anna Briggs; Rev. Dr Cleaves and his wife; Jean Lacock, Cheltenham Local History Society Chairman; and representatives from Countryside Properties.

HECTOR CAFFIERI (1847-1932)
Artist
21 Prestbury Road (map 3 no.16)

Hector Caffieri, a notable Victorian artist, was born at 3 Portland Place, Cheltenham on 7 June 1847. He was the elder son of Philippe Caffieri, a French wine merchant, whose business premises, known as the Montpellier Wine Vaults, were situated in Montpellier Walk, with frontages on both the Walk and Montpellier Street behind.

After being educated in Cheltenham, Hector Caffieri studied art in Paris under Léon Bonnat and Jules-Joseph Lefebvre, both traditional academic artists, before dividing his working life between London and Boulogne-sur-Mer in northern France.

9 - Hector Caffieri

He won acclaim as a prolific painter of landscapes, beach and harbour scenes, still-life and some sporting scenes. Many of his works were charming studies of people on the coast and in the country. Intriguingly he is also said to have covered the Russo-Turkish War of 1877-8.

10 - 'Boulogne Harbour' by Hector Caffieri

Hector Caffieri exhibited his work widely in Britain, and at the Salon de la Société des Artistes Francais, Paris from 1892-93. He was elected a member of the Royal Institute of Painters in Water Colour in 1885 and of the Royal Institute of Painters in Oils in 1894. He was a member of the Royal Society of British Artists and of the New Water Colour Society; he also exhibited some 38 works at the Royal Academy from 1875-1901. His painting *Boulogne Harbour* resides in the Cheltenham Art Gallery and Museum collection.

Hector Caffieri lived at Hampstead Road and Great Russell Street, London from 1882 until at least 1901. He returned to France in 1903 and lived in Boulogne until his death in January 1932.

Many of Hector Caffieri's works have been reprinted as greetings cards by the Medici Society. Sheila Milner developed a great interest in these cards and following her discovery of a small stained glass window in the Lady Chapel of St Gregory's Catholic Church, a memorial to Hector's grandparents, she suggested to David Phillips, Chairman of the Civic Society, that a plaque should be erected to commemorate the artist's birthplace. The Medici Society agreed to co-sponsor the commemorative plaque to Hector Caffieri.

It is not often that plaques are associated with real family occasions, but this was certainly the case when Michael Tupper, the grandson of Hector Caffieri, supported by a dozen other descendants of the artist, unveiled the plaque at 21 Prestbury Road (now Smith & Mann), believed to have been Caffieri's birthplace, on 15 February 1986. The *Gloucestershire Echo* reported the ceremony, and published a photograph of the smiling family group posing on either side of the plaque (see p.56).

At the time that the plaque was unveiled its location at the town end of Prestbury Road was known as Portland Place. It was not until many years later that it was discovered that Hector Caffieri's birthplace was, in fact, a house located where the North Place car park exists today. The plaque is therefore wrongly sited, but surely Hector would not have minded?

11 - 21 Prestbury Road, site of Hector Caffieri's plaque

CECIL DAY LEWIS (1904-72)
Poet Laureate
Box Cottage, Bafford Lane, Charlton Kings
(map 8 no.49)

12 - Cecil Day Lewis at Cheltenham College Junior School, 1935

Box Cottage, Charlton Kings, was the home of the poet Cecil Day Lewis from 1933 until 1938 while he was assistant master at Cheltenham College Junior School.

Cecil Day Lewis was born in Ireland, the son of a parson, and was brought up in London. He was educated at Sherborne School and graduated from Wadham College Oxford in 1927. Related to Irish writer and poet Oliver Goldsmith on his mother's side, he became one of W.H. Auden's poetic 'gang', which also included Stephen Spender and Louis McNiece. He co-operated with W.H. Auden in producing Oxford Poetry (1927).

In his youth Cecil Day Lewis had had communist sympathies and was a member of the Communist party between 1933 and 1938. National Archive records have recently revealed that he was under surveillance by Gloucestershire police in 1933 while living in Cheltenham, after correspondence had been intercepted between himself and Harry Pollitt, head of the Communist Party of Great Britain. However MI5 did not consider him to be a threat to national security and decided that there was no justification for seeking a Home Office warrant.

During World War II Day Lewis worked at the Ministry of Information. It was said that in the 1940s he reached his full stature as a poet. In 1946 he was a lecturer at Cambridge and later taught poetry at Oxford, and was Professor of Poetry there from 1951 to 1956. He received an OBE in 1950 and married his second wife actress Jill Balcon in 1951. He became Poet Laureate in 1968, succeeding John Masefield.

Cecil Day Lewis returned to Cheltenham as guest of honour to read a selection of contemporary verse at the first Cheltenham Literature Festival in 1949. He continued to support the Festival until his death on 22 May 1972. He was buried in Stinsford, Dorset, close to Thomas Hardy, whom he greatly admired.

When actress Jill Balcon unveiled her husband's plaque on Box Cottage on 8 October 1983 she said that if the roof had not leaked, and he had urgently needed £100 for repair, he would never have become a successful novelist. Day Lewis's first novel, *A Question of Proof,* written under the pseudonym of Nicholas Blake, had caused quite a stir in the town. The school featured in the novel was obviously Cheltenham

13 and 14 - Box Cottage, home to Cecil Day Lewis for 5 years

College Junior School, and the lady with whom the hero had an affair was identified as the wife of the headmaster Mr Roseveare. The story was looked on with disapproval by College authorities and he resigned in 1938.

The blue commemorative plaque to Cecil Day Lewis, co-sponsored by Cheltenham College, is affixed to the front of Box Cottage and is visible through the gate (see above). There is no need to enter the garden.

I close the book,
And the past slides out of its leaves to haunt me
And it seems, wherever I look
Phantoms of irreclaimable happiness taunt me.
From The Album by Cecil Day Lewis (1943)

Daniel Day Lewis, second child of Cecil Day Lewis and Jill Balcon, is a renowned actor of both stage and screen. His brilliant performance as Christy Brown in Jim Sheridan's film *My Left Foot* won him numerous awards, including an Oscar for Best Actor in 1989.

SIR GEORGE DOWTY (1901-74)
Aeronautical Engineer
Mews End, 10 Lansdown Terrace Lane (map 6 no.46)

In 1962 L.T.C. Rolt published *The Dowty Story,* tracing the story of the Dowty Group from 1931 onwards, with a second volume produced in 1973. And what a story it was.

George Herbert Dowty was born in Pershore, Worcestershire and was sent to Worcester Royal Grammar School after losing his right eye at the age of 12 while making a firework. He was apprenticed to the Worcester engineers Heenan and Froude in 1915 and attended evening classes at the Polytechnic Institute. He progressed rapidly through the machine shop, erecting shop, test bed, view room and finally to the drawing office.

15 - Sir George Dowty

In 1918 George Dowty began working as a draughtsman at A.V. Roe before joining the Gloster Aircraft Company (GAC) in 1924. He became an expert in undercarriage design, and was granted a full patent on his design for an internally sprung landing-wheel in January 1929. When in 1931 GAC could not respond to a request from a Japanese aircraft constructor for six internally sprung wheels, George decided he could produce them himself. Resigning from Gloster Aircraft he rented a loft at 10 Lansdown Terrace Lane at 2s 6d a week, employed himself at £3 a week, and engaged two craftsmen who worked in the evenings. Together they fulfilled the order.

The lack of space in his tiny workshop forced George Dowty to move to premises in Grosvenor Street South under the name of Aircraft Components Co. Despite his initial success a lack of further orders forced him to make small articles for a variety of markets - for example metal labels for gardeners and developing dishes for photographers. In 1935 he approached his former employer, A.W.

Martyn of GAC, for financial backing. Martyn, recognising George Dowty's innovative skills and business acumen, immediately arranged a £3,000 guarantee on the company's bank account, followed by a £30,000 cash injection for expansion, which included the purchase of Arle Court where the Dowty Group developed.

In only four years Dowty's had orders worth £10 million and had opened two more factories in Canada and the USA. By the end of World War II the company had produced nearly a million hydraulic units and 87,000 retractable undercarriages for numerous aircraft including Lancasters, Hurricanes, Meteors and the Gloster/Whittle jet aircraft. During the war Dowty's had also established a repair and salvage factory in Ashchurch. A war effort indeed! By the mid-1950s the Dowty Group comprised 25 companies world-wide, including Dowty Seals and Dowty Mining Equipment located at Ashchurch and in 1960 Dowty Equipment Ltd and Rotol Ltd combined to form Dowty Rotol, with factories at Staverton. The Group was by far the largest European manufacturer of aircraft equipment at that time. 40,000 Dowty roofing spats helped keep the roof on the former Wembley Stadium and Dowty pit props were used to support London's spectacular Victorian Olympia Grand Hall after wooden supports gave way.

George Dowty became an Honorary Freeman of the Borough of Cheltenham in 1955, and was also a Freeman of both Gloucester and Tewkesbury. He received a knighthood in 1956 for his services to industry. He was President of the Royal Aeronautical Society from 1952-3, President of the Society of British Aircraft

16 - 10 Lansdown Terrace Lane

Constructors from 1960-1 and in 1971 was made Master of the Worshipful Company of Coach Makers. He died at his home on the Isle of Man on 7 December 1974, at the age of 74. On 4 April 1987 Sir Robert Hunt unveiled the blue plaque to Sir George Dowty at 10 Lansdown Terrace Lane in pouring rain in the presence of Society Chairman, David Phillips. Sir Robert, Dowty's first apprentice in the 1930s, was Chairman of the Dowty Group until his retirement in 1986. The Group co-sponsored the plaque (see p.13).

JOHN GODING (1816-79)
Cheltenham Historian
3 Portland Street (map 3 no.18)

17 - John Goding

The historian John Goding wrote the first comprehensive history of Cheltenham, named *Norman's History of Cheltenham* after its publisher George Norman. The first edition was printed in 1853. The extended second edition, published ten years later, is still often consulted by historians today and is packed with a wealth of facts about the town gathered from many other earlier sources, many of which are no longer available. Goding lived at 3 Portland Street (now the Everest Indian restaurant) from 1835-74.

John Goding was born in London and moved with his parents to Cheltenham when he was about 12. His father opened a grocery store in Burton Street. It is not known which school John attended, but it is recorded that he was an intelligent boy with a thirst for knowledge.

There is a portrait of John Goding in the Cheltenham Art Gallery and Museum collection (above). The portrait shows him wearing a ring engraved with the name of his favourite daughter Amelia.

When he was a little older John Goding attended lectures at the Mechanics Institute, which stood in Albion Street, and he was later to lecture there himself. It was at this Institute that he became friendly with Unitarian Mr Furber. It was through the efforts of Mr Furber, John Goding and 'other energetic spirits' that the Bayshill Unitarian Church was opened in 1844. Goding became a Unitarian himself, and it may have been his research into the Unitarian movement in Cheltenham that had led him to write a history of the town.

In 1865 John Goding became Assistant Overseer as collector of the poor rate. Allegations, largely unfounded, regarding his compilation of the Electoral Roll may have hastened his death at the age of 63. At the weekly meeting of the Board of Guardians following John Goding's death there were glowing tributes, and it was pointed out that he had left the books in order all ready for the collection of the new rate. One Guardian said:

'He was a citizen of no mean order and a man of considerable culture and painstaking research after knowledge'.

Appropriately Cheltenham Local History Society co-sponsored the blue commemorative plaque at 3 Portland Street to commemorate the life and work of John Goding. The late Jean Laycock, then Chairman of Cheltenham Local History Society, was present when the Mayor, Councillor Les Freeman, unveiled the plaque on 14 October 1995. John Goding would have been pleased to know that the Minister and the Chairman of Bayshill Unitarian Church had shared in the ceremony.

In 1965 well-known local historian Gwen Hart paid tribute to John Goding in the preface to her *A History of Cheltenham,* the first comprehensive history of the town since Goding's in 1891:

'Although he was untrained ... as a historian, he was the only writer of his generation in Cheltenham who realised the importance of the sources then available: the Cheltenham [Manor] *Court Books, the Vestry Books, and the collection of documents made in the eighteenth century ...* [His work] *is a most valuable source book to which I am deeply indebted.'*

18 - 3 Portland Street

MARIE HALL (1884-1956)
International Violinist
Broadleas, 9 Eldorado Road (map 6 no.43)

19 - Marie Hall, about 1905

Marie Hall was considered the foremost British woman violinist during the first half of the 20th century. She was born Mary Paulina Hall in Newcastle-upon-Tyne in 1884, but lived in Cheltenham from 1911 until her death in the town in 1956.

Marie Hall received her first music lessons from her father, who was a harpist in the orchestra of the Carl Rosa Opera Company. A child prodigy, she was recommended for the Royal Academy of Music, London when she was just nine years of age. She studied under Elgar for a year, and then spent three years in Birmingham with Max Mosel, before moving to the Prague Conservatoire. She made her first professional appearance in Prague in November 1902 at the age of 18, and her London debut on 16 February the following year. Despite her frail appearance she was soon engaged on long tours world-wide and performed strenuous musical programmes, apparently without fatigue.

Renowned British composer Ralph Vaughan Williams composed *The Lark Ascending* for Marie and dedicated it to her. This popular musical piece, based on English folk themes and a poem by George Meredith, features a prominent solo violin part which conveys the beauty of a skylark rising into the heavens above a typical sunny English scene, attaining such height that it becomes barely visible to those below. Marie gave the first public performance of the piece at the Queen's Hall, London under conductor Adrian Boult in 1921.

Marie Hall married her agent Edward Baring in London in January 1911, and it is an indication of her international reputation that this event was reported in *The New York Times*.

The couple moved to 9 Eldorado Road, Cheltenham the same year and their daughter Pauline was born in Cheltenham in 1912. Pauline Baring was a talented pianist, and she and her mother performed together on many occasions, including giving recitals on BBC radio.

Marie Hall bought what is known as the Viotti Stradivarius for £1,600 in 1905, and it became her only concert violin until her death in 1956. The instrument, made in 1709 and described as 'a perfect Stradivarius in every respect', was sold by Pauline Baring at Sotheby's, London in 1968 for what was then a record £22,000. The violin was purchased by the Royal Academy of Music for £3.5 million in 2005, and is now among the instruments exhibited in the Ashmolean Museum, Oxford.

Marie Hall continued to live at 9 Eldorado Road after her husband's death in 1951 until her own death on 11 November 1956. Her funeral was held at Christ Church, Malvern Road. She left £1,000 to what is now known as the Cheltenham Music Festival, in memory of her husband's long association with it. The Festival, first held just three weeks after the end of World War II, continues to this day and attracts musicians from all over the world. Pauline Baring continued living in Eldorado Road until her death in 1971. She was buried in Cheltenham Borough cemetery in the same grave as her parents. Pauline was a member of Cheltenham Civic Society, and in appreciation of a small legacy a room in Parmoor House was dedicated to her memory.

Ursula, widow of composer Ralph Vaughan Williams, unveiled the blue commemorative plaque to Marie Hall at 9 Eldorado Road on 9 June 1984. At the ceremony David Phillips, Chairman of the Civic Society, was accompanied by John Yarnley, local representative of the Incorporated Society of Musicians, co-sponsors of the plaque.

The owner of 9 Eldorado Road, which is now a rest home, was very pleased to have the plaque refurbished in 2002.

20 - 9 Eldorado Road

SIR FREDERICK HANDLEY PAGE (1885-1962)
Aeronautical Engineer
Cranham Villa, 3 King's Road. (map 4 no.24)

21 - Frederick Handley Page

Frederick Handley Page, one of the greatest aircraft designers of the 20th century, was born at 3 King's Road, Cheltenham on 15 November 1885, the son of an upholsterer. He was educated at Cheltenham Grammar School.

In 1902 Handley Page began studying electrical engineering in London. Upon graduation in 1906 he became an engineer with a small electrical manufacturer. By the age of 21 he was chief designer of the company. He became fascinated by aircraft and built and flew several experimental biplanes and monoplanes. In 1908 he set up as an aeronautical engineer and on 17 June 1909 he registered his first company, Handley Page Ltd., in Barking, Essex, with a capital of £10,000, establishing the first public British company ever to build aircraft - he was then only 24.

In 1914 Handley Page won a contract to build bomber biplanes for the Royal Navy and designed the O/100 heavy bomber, which first flew in December 1915 and became Britain's standard bomber in World War I. At the time it was the largest aircraft to have been built in the UK and one of the largest in the world. Recognising the long-range transport value of large

22 - Handley Page O/100.
Royal Naval Air Service, 1918

aircraft, Handley Page founded Handley Page Transport Ltd. in 1919 and with it opened routes to Paris and Amsterdam. This company became Imperial Airways, later renamed British Overseas Airways Corporation (BOAC) and today known as British Airways.

The first Handley Page Halifax bomber was assembled in October 1939. The Halifax, named after the then Foreign Secretary, played a major role in World War II, and Handley Page bombers were converted to transport planes for the Berlin airlift in 1948-9. One of the last complete Halifax bombers can be seen at the Yorkshire Air Museum, Elvington, Yorkshire, an old RAF base. The Handley Page Victor was a strategic bomber jet aircraft, first flown in 1952 and in active service with the RAF from 1957 to 1965. The Victor, together with the Avro Vulcan and the Vickers Valiant, were originally designed for high speed, high altitude penetration of Soviet air space. Collectively known as the 'V' bombers, these three aircraft provided Britain's nuclear deterrent during the 1950s until the mid-1960s. After 1965 the Victor continued in service as a tanker aircraft until it was formally retired in 1993.

From 1909 until Frederick Handley Page's death in 1962, 63 types of aircraft bore his name. At the peak of production 41 factories and dispersal units with 600 sub-contractors and 51,000 employees produced one aircraft every hour. He was awarded a CBE in 1918 and a knighthood in 1942. He was President of the Royal Aeronautical Society from 1945-7 and was awarded the Gold Medal of the Royal Aeronautical Society in 1960. He is believed to have helped set up the RAF Cranwell College of Aeronautics in November 1919, the oldest military air academy in the world, and held the position of Lord Lieutenant of Middlesex from 1956-60.

*23 - Cranham Villa,
3 King's Road*

In 1982 Phil Newcombe, then the Cheltenham Civic Society Secretary, received a letter from the Handley Page Association, asking for a plaque to be erected on Sir Frederick Handley Page's birthplace at 3 Kings Road to celebrate the 20th anniversary of the engineer's death. The Handley Page Association agreed to bear half the cost, and the plaque erected became the first Civic Society plaque in the town. It was unveiled by his daughter, Mrs Manley Walker from Cirencester, on 22 April 1982, in the presence of the Mayor and David Phillips, Chairman of the Society.

SIR ARTHUR HARRIS (1892-1984)
Marshall of the RAF
3 Queen's Parade (map 5 no.34)

24 - Sir Arthur Harris

On 19 September 1982 Sir Arthur Travers Harris, known to many as 'Bomber' Harris, unveiled a plaque on his birthplace, 3 Queen's Parade. He had come at the invitation of Cheltenham Civic Society and the local branch of the RAF Association, who had co-sponsored the plaque. At the ceremony Harris told Phil Newcombe of the Civic Society that this was the first time he had returned to Cheltenham in the 20th century, and that his one abiding memory of the house was the squawking of the parrot next door.

Arthur Harris was born at 3 Queen's Parade on 13 April 1892 while his parents were on leave from India. His father was a civil servant and his mother was the daughter of an Army physician in Madras. Arthur spent only two years at kindergarten in Cheltenham before being sent to Gore Court School, Sittingbourne, Kent and then to All Hallows, Honiton, Devon. He left school when he was 16 and emigrated to Rhodesia where he worked as a tobacco planter, coach driver and miner. In 1914 he joined the 1st Rhodesian Regiment as a bugler, transferring to the Royal Flying Corps in 1915.

Arthur Harris served as a Squadron Commander in India and Iraq after World War I. He was made Group Captain in 1933, was appointed Director of Planning in the Air Ministry 1934-7, and served as Assistant Officer Commanding, 5 Bomber Group from 1939-40. As Commander-in-Chief Bomber Command from 1942-5 he was architect of all the '1,000 bomber' and subsequent raids over Germany of which there has been much criticism in hindsight. Harris was made Marshall of the RAF in 1946 and retired the following year. In 1953 Prime Minister Winston Churchill insisted that he accept a baronetcy, and he became Sir Arthur Travers Harris, 1st Baronet of Chipping Wycombe.

25 - Avro Lancaster Mark 1

Sir Arthur Harris died at Goring-on-Thames, Oxfordshire on 5 April 1984 at the age of 91. The Parish Church service was attended mainly by family and friends and a few old comrades. He was interred at Burwood cemetery, a few miles away in Surrey, where other RAF personnel are also buried. A lone Lancaster, flying very low, was the RAF's closing tribute. In a special RAF stamp issue in September 1986 Sir Arthur Harris was featured beside a Lancaster on the 31p stamp. A statue to Harris was unveiled outside the RAF chapel, St Clement Danes, London in 1992.

26 - 3 Queen's Parade, Montpellier

DR EDWARD JENNER (1749-1823)
Pioneer of Vaccination
22 St George's Place (map 1 no.4)

27 - Dr Edward Jenner

Amongst the many achievements associated with the men and women of Cheltenham, Dr Edward Jenner's work on vaccination against smallpox must surely have had the greatest effect on the world. In 1980 the World Health Organisation certified the elimination of smallpox, the only human infectious disease to have been completely eradicated from nature.

Edward Jenner born in Berkeley, Gloucestershire, was the youngest son of the parish Vicar. He began his medical studies at the age of 14 and, after studying surgery and anatomy at St George's Hospital, University of London, he returned to Gloucestershire to become a country doctor. He carried out extensive studies of plant and animal life and, as a result, was offered a place on Captain James Cook's second voyage (1772-5), but did not accept. He became a Fellow of the Royal Society in 1788.

In 1795 Jenner and his family took lodgings opposite a druggist's shop in Cheltenham's Lower High Street. They moved to 8 St George's Place (now no. 22) the following year, living there on a seasonal basis. That part of St George's Place was known locally as Harley Street at that time because at least four doctors lived there.

Jenner knew of the country belief that those who caught cowpox, a mild disease, would never catch smallpox. He reasoned that if he could transmit cowpox from one person to another, he could protect them from smallpox. In 1776 he introduced fluid extracted from a cowpox pustule on a milkmaid's skin under the skin of James Phipps, the 8 year old son of a local labourer. He was able to show that the boy was immune to smallpox, calling his method 'vaccination' from 'vacca', the Latin word for cow. He did not understand how vaccination worked, but his scientific investigations showed that using fluid from a human with cowpox was safer than the alternative, known as 'variolation', which involved inoculating non-infected people with fluid from smallpox pustules. He eventually published several papers on his method, the first of which was *Inquiry into the Cause and Effects of Variolae Vaccinae* [cow-pox] in 1798.

Jenner offered free vaccinations to the poor at Alpha House, St George's Road (currently part of Spirax Sarco) during a smallpox outbreak in 1800. Called 'the Pest House' by the locals, Alpha House was an old farmhouse belonging to surgeon, Thomas Cother. A Public Libraries Committee plaque to Dr Edward Jenner can be seen on Alpha House. See p.100 for further details.

Dr Edward Jenner retired to The Chantry, Berkeley, following the death of his wife in 1815, and lived there until his death in 1823. His friend the Rev. Robert Ferryman built the rustic thatched 'Temple of Vaccinia' in the garden. It was here that Edward Jenner vaccinated the poor people of the district, without charge. It is internationally important for its historical and architectural interest. The Chantry and garden now house the Edward Jenner Museum.

The blue plaque to Dr Edward Jenner was erected on 22 St George's Place, a reproduction of the original house which stood on the site. 22 and 24 St George's Place contain eight flats, let at affordable rents to single people through the Borough Council's Housing Needs Register, and developed by Sovereign Housing Association, which co-sponsored the plaque. The plaque was unveiled on 20 April 1995 by the Mayor, Councillor Deborah Griggs.

Opposite 22 St George's Place is the site of the original gardens for Jenner's house. Jenner Gardens, later the graveyard for Cheltenham Chapel, is currently being restored to honour this medical pioneer (2008). See website for details (www.friends-of-jenner-gardens.org.uk).

28 - 22 St George's Place, the site of Jenner's home

BRIAN JONES (1942-69)
Rock Musician
Rosemead, 17 Eldorado Road (map 6 no.42)

29 - Brian Jones

To some, Brian Jones, founder of the Rolling Stones rock group, was a controversial figure, but when his fan club raised sponsorship money for a plaque on his family home in Eldorado Road the Civic Society agreed to their request.

Brian Jones was born in Park Nursing Home, Cheltenham on 28 February 1942, the son of Lewis Blount Jones and his wife Louisa. The family lived at Rosemead, 17 Eldorado Road from 1942 to 1950, before moving to Hatherley Road. Brian attended Dean Close Junior School from 1947-53 and then Cheltenham Grammar School at its former High Street site (1953-9). In the early 1960s he spent over a year working at the County Architect's Office, Gloucester, as a trainee.

In addition to his job as an aeronautical engineer with Dowty's, Jones's father Lewis played both piano and organ, and led the choir at the local church. His mother Louisa was a piano teacher and started teaching her son the instrument at a very young age.

Arnold J. Berkman, Vice-President of the Brian Jones Fan Club, describes how Brian's name will always be associated with The Rolling Stones:

'He started piano lessons when six years old and later played the clarinet in [the] school orchestra, When he was 16 he sold the clarinet for a second-hand alto saxophone, (as played by his idol Charlie 'Bird' Parker). He then quickly taught himself to play guitar and slide guitar and became a member of two local groups: 'The Cheltenham 6' and 'The Ramrods'. He also learnt the harmonica. By the time he founded 'The Rolling Stones' he could play 30 instruments. The band was first called 'The Rollin' Stones', derived from a song by Muddy Waters, but later 'The Rolling Stones'.

Success came quickly for the band and Brian Jones lived the rock star lifestyle to the full. Tragically he was found drowned in the pool at his Sussex mansion on 3 July 1969, despite being a strong swimmer. The coroner's report concluded that it was 'death by misadventure', but noted that his liver and heart had been heavily enlarged by drug and alcohol abuse. He was only 27.

Brian Jones's funeral was held at St. Mary's Parish Church, Cheltenham on 10 July 1969 and he was buried in Cheltenham cemetery, Bouncer's Lane, in a prominent position at the corner of the path leading to the Crematorium chapel, in a lavish silver and bronze casket given by his friend, Bob Dylan. Brian's Fan Club members come to Cheltenham from many countries, especially Japan, anxious to visit every site in the town associated with their hero. His grave is said never to be without flowers.

On 3 July 2003, the 34th anniversary of Brian Jones's death, Nigel Jones MP for Cheltenham, was welcomed by John Henry, Chairman of the Civic Society, and unveiled the plaque on the entrance to 17 Eldorado Road. Among the many fans were Brian's girlfriend, Pat Andrews, and his former flatmate Richard Hattrell.

*30 - Rosemead,
17 Eldorado Road*

The *Gloucestershire Echo*, which had championed the initial proposal for the plaque, gave special coverage to the event. It was John Henry and the Fan Club who made everything happen, with the support of Mr and Mrs Duncan, the owners of no. 17. The unveiling culminated in a party at the house.

HERBERT HENRY MARTYN (1842-1937)
Architectural Art Worker and Philanthropist
Stirling Court, Corner of High Street & College Road
(map 4 no.21)

31 - H.H. Martyn, 1918, aged 76

The plaque to Herbert Henry Martyn is considered by many to be one of the most important that the Civic Society has erected in the town. Born in poverty Herbert Martyn, often referred to as H.H. Martyn, grew up in Worcester. He had several menial jobs before being apprenticed to James Forsyth, an architectural sculptor. Later he joined another carver, R.L. Boulton, and when Boulton's studio moved to Cheltenham Martyn followed. He formed a partnership with Mr E.A. Emms, stonemason, two years later. In 1888 he founded H.H. Martyn, Architectural Carvers, at premises named Sunningend at the corner of the High Street and College Road. The rear of Sunningend, for many years a Rolls Royce car showroom, has recently been rebuilt and is now known as Stirling Court.

By 1920 H.H. Martyn had 1,000 employees producing carvings in wood, stone and metal. They also produced decorative plasterwork, wrought iron, stained glass, large scale bronze castings, cabinet making and joinery and their fine workmanship became known worldwide. They were responsible for some of the nation's finest architectural art work, including the pulpit in St Paul's Cathedral, the Speaker's Chair and dispatch boxes in the House of Commons, Buckingham Palace Long Gallery, the Whitehall Cenotaph, the Menin Gate, Ypres and dozens of European war memorials. In Cheltenham there are wonderful

32 - Sunningend, High Street c.1890

carvings in wood and stone in Cheltenham College Chapel, the Ladies' College and many churches. Martyn's decorative work extended to fitting out all the leading liners and passenger ships of the day, including all the Queen liners, the *Titanic* and the *Lusitania.*

In 1908 H.H. Martyn moved into the Trusty Engine Works (and neighbouring Vulcan Iron Works), near Lansdown railway station, renaming these premises Sunningend. During World War I the company made aircraft fuselages and in 1917 Alfred W. Martyn, H.H. Martyn's son, formed the Gloucester (later Gloster) Aircraft Company (GAC). George Dowty joined the drawing office of the company in 1924. Alfred Martyn helped Dowty to establish a company of his own in 1935 and became Dowty's Company Chairman in 1936. See p.22.

33 - Stirling Court

H.H. Martyn died in 1937 and in an obituary he was described as both an artist and social worker. In 1870 he had been supportive in opening a mission for the poor near the Lower High Street and established a Temperance Society there. Then in 1883 he founded the Working Men's College over a bookshop in Clarence Street. When Miss Beale, Principal of Cheltenham Ladies' College, opened his college, she suggested that one day their two colleges might amalgamate to form a famous university. It was not to be, but Martyn's college was the forerunner of the North Gloucestershire Technical College, now Gloucestershire College.

In 1985 John Whittaker, great-grandson of H.H. Martyn, published *The Best,* which told the story of Martyn's with many pages of illustrations of their work. On 2 April 2005 Mayor, Councillor Rob Garnham, unveiled the blue plaque on Stirling Court. Phil Newcombe officiated at the ceremony on a windy, sunny, Saturday morning, in the presence of members of the Civic Society and the Cheltenham Local History Society, as well as Keith Bawden, one of Martyn's former craftsmen. John Whittaker, who co-sponsored the plaque, presented the Mayor with a copy of *The Best.* After the ceremony guests were entertained by Messrs Willis, present occupiers of Stirling Court.

JOHN NEVIL MASKELYNE (1839-1917)
Illusionist and Watchmaker
12 Rotunda Terrace, Montpellier (map 5 no.32)

34 - John Nevil Maskelyne

The name Maskelyne is familiar to illusionists and magic historians across the world. John Nevil Maskelyne, the first of three generations of illusionists who bore the name, was born at 20 White Hart Row, now White Hart Street, off the Lower High Street, Cheltenham, the son of a saddler and publican.

Growing up in Cheltenham J.N. Maskelyne, as he was known professionally, was said to have been '...*a youth with natural aptitude for scientific research and a perfect mastery of mechanical resources*'. To develop his talents Maskelyne's father apprenticed him to Frederick M. Brown, 'Jeweller, silversmith and watchmaker' of Winchcombe Street and 4 Montpellier Walk. By 1861 Maskelyne had completed his apprenticeship and set up in business at 12 Rotunda Terrace, Montpellier. At that time he was living at that address with his family, including six of his seven surviving sisters. He married Elizabeth Taylor, a Cheltenham girl, on 10 December 1862 at Swindon Village Parish Church.

John Nevil Maskelyne had been interested in magic from an early age, and formed a conjuring club with half a dozen friends, meeting at each other's houses and developing simple mechanisms to create illusions. On 7 March 1865 Maskelyne watched a performance by the American spiritualists known as the Davenport Brothers at the old Town Hall, Regent Street, with great interest. A few weeks later he announced in the local newspapers that he and his friend George Cooke, a tailor from Burton Street, Cheltenham, would '...*undertake to perform, in open daylight, the tricks which the Davenports professed to accomplish by "spiritual aid"*' at Jessop's Gardens, where Waitrose stands today (see p.87).The show was a great success, and Maskelyne and Cooke toured the country with their act for several years. They gave their first Royal performance before the Prince of Wales at Berkeley Castle in January 1870 and later at the Crystal Palace, London. In 1873 they took out a lease on part of the Egyptian Hall, Piccadilly, London, expecting to stay there a few months. They stayed for over 30 years! In 1904 the company moved to St George's Hall, Langham Place, London. Maskelyne died at St George's Hall on 18 May 1917.

35 - Maskelyne's home & business premises, 12 Rotunda Terrace

In addition to the construction of stage illusions Maskelyne turned his talents to many other inventions, including a coin-operated 'penny-in-the-slot' lock for ladies' toilets, from which we get the British phrase 'to spend a penny'. He also invented two typewriters, a gas burner for a hot air balloon and an automatic bus ticket dispenser. His descendents inherited his innovative skills and the family registered a total of 40 British patents from 1875-1913.

On 10 June 1989 Paul Daniels, well-known British magician and avid collector of Maskelyne memorabilia, unveiled the plaque on 12 Rotunda Terrace. The Mayor, Councillor Eric Phillips, and Chairman Phil Newcombe from the Civic Society were also present (see p.56). The plaque was co-sponsored by Douglas and Jenny Ogle of Ogle Fine Arts, who owned the building. Paul Daniels, accompanied by his wife Debbie McGee, made many humorous quips throughout the ceremony and performed several tricks at the lunch which took place at the Queen's Hotel afterwards.

A second, much earlier plaque to John Nevil Maskelyne, commemorating the site of his exposure of the Davenport Brothers, can be seen in the foyer of the Everyman Theatre, Regent Street (see p.103).

LILLAH MCCARTHY (1875-1960)
Actress
148 High Street (map 2 no.10)

Cheltenham-born actress Lillah McCarthy had the honour of speaking the very first lines on the stage at the opening of the new Shakespeare Memorial Theatre in Stratford-upon-Avon on St George's Day, 23 April 1932. Her appearance came immediately after the Prince of Wales had taken his place in the Royal Box and the National Anthem had been sung.

36 - Lillah McCarthy performed 'The Sign of the Cross' in Cheltenham in Nov 1903

According to *The Times:*
'...the curtain depicting the Stratford of Shakespeare's day rose upon a drop curtain of beautifully blended colours. Through this curtain stepped Miss Lillah McCarthy, a brilliant figure in green and grey velvet to declaim the Poet Laureate's ode and to make the first mark on a new page of history'.

The Poet Laureate John Masefield, a close friend of Lillah's, had written the ode especially for the occasion, recalling the disastrous fire that had destroyed the previous theatre.

Lillah, real name Lila Emma McCarthy, was born on the site of 148 High Street (now Burger King) on 22 September 1875. She was the seventh of eight children of Jonadab McCarthy, Cheltenham antique dealer, and his wife Emma from Worcester. Lillah was educated at home by her doting, if eccentric father. In her autobiography *Myself and my Friends* Lillah recorded that her childhood hero was Gilbert Jessop, the cricketer, who lived in Cambray Place. (See plaque to Jessop on p.85). She also recalled that as a girl she was present when Lillie Langtry had opened the Theatre and Opera House in Cheltenham (now the Everyman Theatre) with a performance of *Lady Clancarty* in 1891.

37 - 148 High Street

Lillah McCarthy showed an early talent for acting, and when she was 18 the family moved to London so that she could study under two of the foremost theatrical teachers of the day. Two years later George Bernard Shaw was very impressed by her performance as Lady Macbeth in an amateur Shakespearean Society production, and she made her name in his plays, becoming one of the best-known actresses of her day. In 1906 she married Harley Granville-Barker continuing her career in plays by Masefield, Galsworthy, J.M. Barry and Ibsen. She and her husband managed The Savoy and St James's theatres, London, where they put on productions of Shakespeare's plays. They toured Australia and the USA, and she appeared in productions on Broadway in 1915. She also appeared in several films.

Sadly Lillah McCarthy and Granville-Barker divorced in 1918. However with encouragement from Bernard Shaw she continued her theatre work. She married botanist Frederick Keeble in 1920, exchanging the world of the theatre for that of science, and only returned to the stage for the occasional recital, including several at Cheltenham Town Hall in 1925. She died in London in 1960. Two portraits of her by Charles Shannon R.A. hang in Cheltenham Art

Gallery and Museum. One shows her as Doña Ana in Shaw's *Man and Superman,* and the other as the Dumb Wife in Anatole France's *The Man who Married a Dumb Wife* (see right).

Lillah McCarthy's plaque was unveiled on 148 High Street on 7 September 1985 by Don Mickley, Chairman of the Cheltenham Theatre and Arts Club, which had co-sponsored the plaque. In attendance were the Mayor, Councillor Peter Pennell, and David Phillips, Chairman of the Civic Society.

38 - Lillah McCarthy as 'The Dumb Wife'

SIR RALPH RICHARDSON (1902-83)
Actor
Charnes, 11 Tivoli Road (map 7 no.47)

Ralph Richardson was born at 11 Tivoli Road, Cheltenham six days before Christmas 1902, the son of Arthur Richardson and his wife Lydia. Arthur was Master at the School of Art at the Ladies' College and a Quaker. When Ralph Richardson was four his Catholic mother left his father and moved with her son to Shoreham-by-Sea, raising him in her own faith. They lived in a home made from two disused railway carriages. There they had a nanny who had been in the service of the Bird family, of custard fame, and Richardson joked that he was fed on custard every day.

*39 - Sir Ralph Richardson
1981*

Ralph Richardson attended the Xaverian Brothers' Catholic College in Brighton. He had set his heart on a theatrical career, despite his father's wish that he study art and his mother who wanted him to be a priest. A Brighton theatre offered Richardson the chance to help with scene painting and, in 1921, aged 19 he made his first stage appearance at Lowestoft. In 1924 he joined Birmingham Repertory Theatre, and he made his London West End debut in 1926. He performed on Broadway for the first time in *Romeo and Juliet* in 1935. When the war came he rose to the rank of Lieutenant-Commander in the Royal Naval Volunteer Reserve, but was released in 1944 so he could act and direct drama at the Old Vic Theatre, London.

As well as performing famous stage roles Ralph Richardson made many film appearances, and was Oscar-nominated for *The Heiress* (1949) and posthumously for *Greystoke: the Legend of Tarzan* (1984). He also appeared on radio and television, notably playing Dr Watson opposite John Gielgood as Sherlock Holmes and Orson Welles as Moriarty in the 1954-5 US/UK radio co-production. He was knighted in 1947.

Ralph Richardson maintained his links with Cheltenham throughout his life, opening the first Cheltenham Festival of Literature on 3 October 1949. In typical fashion he described himself as 'a jockey of literature' and continued 'the dramatist writes the plays and we try to make them run.' He toasted the prosperity of the Festival: 'Whenever Cheltenham crops up in conversation I say with over-elaborate carelessness "As a matter of fact I was born there" as if I owned the place.' He was the Mayor's guest of honour at the Festival's inaugural lunch at the Queen's Hotel later that day. Richardson was also President of the Cheltenham Little Theatre Company, and an Everyman Theatre studio is named after him.

An enthusiastic and fearless motor cyclist well into his 70s, Ralph Richardson relished life. In 1976 he proposed that a firework be launched from the roof of the newly-opened National Theatre, on the South Bank, London on every first night. He was delighted when his proposal was accepted. 'I love fireworks' he said, 'they're so unnecessary'. Unfortunately the practice, known as 'Ralph's Rocket', was discontinued when terrorist alerts in the city made it inadvisable.

Sir Ralph Richardson unveiled the Civic Society plaque on his birthplace on 6 November 1982. It was a splendid occasion and the first time a Cheltenham plaque-unveiling ceremony had been televised. Some

40 - Charnes, 11 Tivoli Road

onlookers stood under the tree that he had climbed as a boy, and from which he had surprised passers-by by calling out 'How are you feeling today?' David Phillips, Civic Society Chairman, had invited Sir Ralph to come to Cheltenham. He had agreed, and the National Theatre had co-sponsored the plaque. David Phillips was a prime mover in the re-opening of the Everyman Theatre in 1959. He was also Chairman of the Everyman Theatre and this is recorded on a plaque in his honour in the Everyman.

Sir Ralph Richardson died on 10 October 1983, at the age of 80. He is buried in Highgate Cemetery, London.

GEORGE ROWE (1796-1864)
Artist and Print-maker
3 Priory Terrace (map 4 no.26)

41 - George Rowe at his printing press, as shown in one of his own prints, dated 1841

The bookshelves of local historians are packed ever more tightly with newly-published books on Cheltenham's past. However George Rowe's *Illustrated Cheltenham Guide*, first published in 1845, is still frequently referenced more than 160 years later. Rowe's Guide shows and describes many shops and buildings, some of which have disappeared, and some of which we can still recognise today. A facsimile of the 1850 edition was published in 1969. The *Guide* was reprinted in 1981 with a comprehensive introduction by Dr Steven Blake.

Born in Exeter, George Rowe moved to Cheltenham in about 1832. Already one of the most prolific 19th century English topographical print makers, he and his wife Philippa established a Repository of Arts in St George's Place where they sold prints and artists' materials, and gave drawing lessons. They then moved their business, first to No. 12 Colonnade and then to Grosvenor Street. Over the next 20 years Rowe produced at least 129 lithographic views, about half of which were of Cheltenham. In 1841 he became co-proprietor and publisher of the *Cheltenham Examiner* newspaper. The business was established at 11 Clarence Street under the name of Rowe & Norman. There is a fine illustration of these premises (right) in his *Illustrated Cheltenham Guide,* which was published there.

42 - Rowe & Norman, 11 Clarence Street

George Rowe took a very active part in the life of Cheltenham, which included being the Parish Churchwarden, a Town Commissioner and an overseer of the poor. He was High Bailiff of the Borough of Cheltenham from 1845-6, and was a founder member of the Liberal Association.

In 1848 George Rowe purchased the Royal Old Well with architect Samuel Onley, developer of much of the Bayshill estate. The project was a financial disaster and in 1852 he left England to join the gold rush in Australia, leaving his wife and children in England. He became involved in a variety of activities on the gold-fields including selling goods to diggers, painting sketches of the fields, designing flags for diggers' tents as well as buying and selling gold. Unfortunately poor health plagued him and he did not prosper. However it was in Australia that he produced some very beautiful paintings, one of which won him a medal at the 1862 International Exhibition in London, the only medal awarded to an artist at that event. In Australia he is still well-known for his panoramic views of the Victorian gold-fields and the City of Melbourne. He returned to England in 1859 and spent his last days in Exeter, dying in the city on 2 September 1864, after a protracted illness. He was buried in Heavitree churchyard, east of Exeter. *The Cheltenham Examiner* described him as 'one of the most influential tradesmen of the town'. *The Illustrated Cheltenham Guide* is George Rowe's legacy to Cheltenham.

Between August and October 1982 Cheltenham Art Gallery and Museum mounted an exhibition devoted to Rowe's works, organised by Dr Steven Blake. It brought together examples of Rowe's British and Australian works for the first time, and provided an account of Rowe's 'full and fascinating life'. The accompanying catalogue gives a comprehensive, illustrated account of the exhibits.

43 - 3 Priory Terrace

On 6 October 1984 a commemorative blue plaque was erected to George Rowe on 3 Priory Terrace, where he had lived for several years. The plaque, co-sponsored by the South Western District of the British Printing Industries Federation, was unveiled by Tom Hepplewhite, Branch Chairman of the Federation, in the presence of the Civic Society Chairman, David Phillips.

WILLIAM NASH SKILLICORNE (1807-87)
Cheltenham's First Mayor
Royston, 9 Queen's Parade (map 5 no.33)

It is appropriate that a blue Civic Society plaque commemorates the name Skillicorne since, in many respects, the family gave us the town that we know today.

In 1716 hosier William Mason discovered a mineral spring on his land (now under the Princess Hall, Cheltenham Ladies' College) and began advertising and selling the purgative spa waters. However it was William's

44 - William Nash Skillicorne

son-in-law Henry Skillicorne, a retired Manx sea captain, who really developed the site of the spa from 1738 onwards with his wife Elizabeth, laying out Well Walk, and erecting permanent buildings for dancing and billiards, and 18 'necessary houses' [toilets].

Henry Skillicorne is commemorated in two locations in Cheltenham. He has an extraordinary memorial in St Mary's Parish Church, said to be the longest in the country, and on the far side of the little walled and gated garden behind the Town Hall there is a bust of him in bas-relief by Cheltenham-based sculptor Percy Braisby.

Borough status was conferred on Cheltenham in 1876, and in that year William Nash Skillicorne, great-grandson of Henry Skillicorne, became the first Mayor of the town. He held the office again in 1879. He died in 1887, at the age of 80. Many at that time would have remembered him as a Justice of the Peace, Chairman of the Board of Guardians and as a member of the governing body of the Grammar School.

He was a director of the Assembly Room Company and a director of the Cheltenham Gas Company. William Nash Skillicorne was the son of an Oxford clergyman and lived in the Old Farm in St. George's Place, the home of the Skillicorne family since Henry and Elizabeth first lived there. William moved to 9 Queen's Parade in 1856. Shortly afterwards the Old Farm was demolished and replaced by Shaftesbury Hall, St George's Place (now part of Chelsea Court).

Dr Steven Blake gave a splendid appreciation of both William and Henry Skillicorne at the unveiling of the Civic Society plaque, co-sponsored by Cheltenham Borough Council, at 9 Queen's Parade on 12 June 1999. In Steven Blake's words William Nash Skillicorne '...*was in many ways the classic Victorian "worthy", serving not only as a Councillor and Mayor, but also as Chairman, Treasurer or Trustee of a host of local organisations and societies, particularly in the charitable field.*' Robert Wilson, Chairman of Cheltenham Civic Society, was also present at the ceremony.

45 - Royston, Queen's Parade

William Nash Skillicorne had a son with the same name, who also became Mayor of Cheltenham:

46 - Bust of Henry Skillicorne by Percy Braisby in Skillicorne Gardens

for two years from 1905, and again between 1913-15. Like his father he was very involved with life and charitable works in the town. Sadly he died in a road accident in 1915. Members of the Liberal Club placed a memorial plaque to him on Albion House, North Street in 1917. At the base were the words '*Good Citizen- Faithful Liberal - Steadfast Liberal.*'

So passed the last of the Skillicornes as Mayors of Cheltenham.

SIR ROBERT SMIRKE (1780-1867)
Architect
Montpellier House, 20 Suffolk Square (map 7 no.48)

20 Suffolk Square is situated opposite the club house for Cheltenham Bowling Club. It was here that the renowned architect Sir Robert Smirke spent the last eight years of his life.

Robert Smirke was born in London where his father was a historical painter and book illustrator. Smirke attended Apsley School in Bedfordshire and then was briefly articled to Sir John Soane. He spent four years studying architecture in Italy, Sicily and Greece from the age of 20, and went on to become one of the leading architects of the Greek Revival in Britain.

47 - Sir Robert Smirke

Robert Smirke's first major commission was for Lowther Castle, Cumbria in 1806 at the age of only 25, followed by Eastnor Castle in the Malverns. He built up a large London practice, much of which was concerned with public buildings. In 1807 he became architect to the Board of Trade and was responsible for the greater part of the Royal Mint on Tower Hill, London, built in 1811.

Robert Smirke's two finest works are thought to be the General Post Office in St Martin's-le-Grand, London and the main facade of the British Museum, both of which were started in 1823. In 1829 he was engaged in the reconstruction of the choir at York Minster after a disastrous fire. There followed more London work: the east wing of Somerset House, London Custom House, the College of Physicians, the Carlton Club and many noblemen's mansions. In 1839 he was unsuccessful in a competition for the rebuilding of the Houses of Parliament.

Smirke was a structural innovator; the first British architect to use load-bearing foundations of lime concrete in measured quantities, and one of the first to make use of load-bearing cast-iron beams in public and domestic (as opposed to industrial) architecture.

48 - Shire Hall, Gloucester

Locally Robert Smirke is best-known as the architect of Shire Hall, Gloucester, which opened in 1816 for the county magistrates. His giant Ionic portico remains, as do his polygonal assize courts at the rear, which are still used as Gloucester Crown Court.

Robert Smirke was knighted in 1832 and was awarded the Royal Institute of British Architects' Gold Medal for Architecture in 1853. He moved to Cheltenham in 1859 and died in the town on 18 April 1867. His huge tombstone can be seen in the churchyard of St Peter's, Leckhampton. After his death Smirke's house was a boarding house for Cheltenham Ladies' College for many years, and was renamed Bunwell House.

The blue commemorative plaque to Sir Robert Smirke on 20 Suffolk Square was co-sponsored by Gloucestershire Architectural Association. It was unveiled on 30 April 1983 by the head prefect at Cheltenham Ladies' College, Sue Mei Chew from Kuala Lumpur, in the presence of John Harris, keeper of the Drawings Collection at the Royal Institute of British Architects.

49 - 20 Suffolk Square

RONALD SUMMERFIELD (1916-89)
Antique Collector and Benefactor
21 Bayshill Road (map 5 no.30)

50 - Ronald Summerfield

'Stacked from floor to ceiling' would be an apt description of the shop at the corner of Montpellier Avenue and Montpellier Spa Road (now Pied Piper), and the large decaying house at 21 Bayshill Road owned by eccentric antique dealer Ronald Summerfield.

Summerfield began collecting antiques as a boy in his native Derbyshire, and in 1952 he moved to Cheltenham with his parents, who bought the house in Bayshill Road. He opened his shop in Montpellier and many still remember how reluctant he was to sell any of his antiques. When he suffered a stroke in the flat above his shop in March 1989 he had to be taken out through the window because the stairs were piled high with treasures from his hoard.

Following Ronald Summerfield's death in 1989, at the age of 73, it took 10 men four months to catalogue almost two million items stacked in the two premises, which included pictures, silverware, jewellery, textiles, clocks, ceramics, statues, furniture and books.

Cheltenham Art Gallery and Museum staff were allowed to choose items from his collection and the Friends of Cheltenham Art Gallery and Museum then donated these items to the Museum. The auctions for the remaining house and shop contents were dubbed the 'Sale of the Century'. The auctions, held at Christies, London and Gloucester-based Bruton Knowles

51 - Summerfield's antique shop

over a period of a year, comprised over 14,000 lots and raised nearly seven million pounds.

Fortunately for Cheltenham, under the terms of his will the money raised from the auctions

52 - Dragons racing on Pittville Lake 2003

was put into the Summerfield Charitable Trust, set up three weeks before his death. In the words of the Trust's Chairman, Charles Fisher, the Trust '...*has helped a wide diversity of charities and individuals, often in innovative and unusual ways*' in the Cheltenham area. For example the Summerfield Galleries, at Cheltenham Art Gallery and Museum, were made possible because of the generosity of the Trust. The displays tell the story of how we lived from the earliest times until the reign of Queen Victoria, and include displays on Gloucestershire archaeology and natural history. One of the more unusual donations was to the Cheltenham Samaritans to help fund their first Dragon Boat Racing event in Pittville Park in 2003. The event raised over £11,000.

53 - Summerfield House, showing both Civic Society plaques

In 1999 renovation work began on the house in Bayshill Road. Twelve months later the re-named Summerfield House had been restored and converted into four luxury flats. On 14 April 2000 the blue plaque commemorating this major benefactor to the town was unveiled by Charles Fisher. The ceremony took place in the presence of the Mayor, Councillor David Banyard. Among the guests was Simon Chorley of Bruton Knowles, one of the first people to enter the house after Ronald Summerfield's death. A little later the same year John Henry, Chairman of the Civic Society, unveiled a Civic Award plaque for 'the restoration of a period building' near the blue plaque.

HUGO VAN WADENOYEN (1892-1959)
Photographer
79 Promenade (map 5 no.36)

54 - Hugo Van Wadenoyen

Hugo van Wadenoyen has been hailed as an influential figure in the genesis of British fine art photography, especially in the period from 1945-65 before photography was considered to be an art form. He lived and worked in Cheltenham from 1933 until his death in 1959.

Wadenoyen, whose family was Dutch, trained in art and had originally intended to be an architect. However when his father, an amateur photographer, opened a professional studio in Cardiff in 1914, Wadenoyen followed suit. His photographs were soon being exhibited all over the world and he was made a Fellow of the Royal Photographic Society in 1918. He then worked for the photographers H.J. Whitlock and Sons at their branches in Birmingham, Wolverhampton and London, returning to the Whiteway International Community between Cheltenham and Stroud where he lived with his brother Jakob, and in which he had long had an interest. Very soon he started his own business at several locations in Cheltenham before settling at 79 Promenade.

A generation of Cheltenham residents and visitors to the town had their photographs taken at Studio Hugo. Hugo van Wadenoyen's photographic portraits were characterised by their informality and were a stark contrast to the formal poses that had prevailed before his time. He specialised in lively character studies of children. From his studio he ventured into the town and country. His photographs of Cheltenham are a unique record of the town at that time.

In 1945 Hugo led the 'Combined Societies', a progressive group of photographic societies from Hereford, Wolverhampton and Bristol that broke away from the Royal Photographic Society. He published a series of books on photography. His *Wayside Snapshots*, published in 1947, demonstrated his fresh and very personal approach. 79 Promenade became part of the Municipal Offices in 1956, and Studio Hugo moved to 34

55 - 'Ladies in the Promenade'
by Hugo van Wadenoyen

Rodney Road. However, because of his failing health and eyesight Hugo was rarely there, preferring to spend much of his time at the Whiteway Community. He died in Cheltenham General Hospital on 1 March 1959, aged 67.

In 1998 David Ross, retired Borough Architect, suggested that there should be a plaque to commemorate Hugo van Wadenoyen's life and work in Cheltenham. The Civic Society agreed and Cheltenham Camera Club co-sponsored the plaque. On 13 June 1998 Richard McLeary, Cheltenham Camera Club Chairman, unveiled the plaque at 79 Promenade attended by Civic Society

56 - 79 Promenade

Chairman Robert Wilson. Also at the ceremony was Eric Franks, a fellow member of the Camera Club and well-known local photographer, and June Radford, a member of Cheltenham Civic Society in the 1960s. June had commissioned Wadenoyen many years earlier to photograph her family and he had stayed with them, taking photographs in their familiar surroundings. Cheltenham Art Gallery and Museum mounted an exhibition of Wadenoyen's work from October 1992 to January 1993. Colin Osman, Honorary Fellow of the Royal Society of Photographers and a prominent member of Cheltenham Camera Club, helped to arrange the exhibition.

SIR NORMAN WISDOM O.B.E. (1915-)
Comedian Actor Singer
Hotel du Vin, Parabola Road (map 5 no.28)

57 - Norman Wisdom 2005

'Comedian Actor Singer' were the words that Sir Norman Wisdom asked the Civic Society to put on the plaque on the then Carlton Hotel, Parabola Road that commemorates his war-time days in Cheltenham with the Royal Corps of Signals.

Born in London in 1915 Norman Wisdom's first childhood recollection was of sitting on a step, looking at the sky and seeing a German Zeppelin. As a boy he had a very hard life after his mother left, when he was nine. At one time he became a cabin boy and the seamen taught him how to box. He then joined the 10th Hussars as a bandsman, serving with them in India. Wanting to return to civilian life he was able to buy himself out and became a switchboard operator on a London telephone exchange. When war broke out it was some time before he could obtain release and join the Royal Corps of Signals.

In 1943 Norman Wisdom was billeted at the Moray House Hotel, later the Carlton Hotel (currently the Hotel du Vin), with No. 2 Company War Office Signals. The top secret establishment in Cheltenham was known as 'CWW - Cheltenham Network'. In his autobiography *Don't Laugh at Me* Norman Wisdom records that the Commanding Officer suggested that it would be a good idea to have a dance band. Wisdom could play the saxophone and the clarinet and he picked six other players to form the band. Later the band played at a charity concert in Cheltenham Town Hall. The internationally-acclaimed British actor Rex Harrison was in the audience, and backstage after the show he asked Wisdom whether he was a professional musician. When he said that he was not, Rex Harrison replied 'If you don't give it a try, you must be utterly mad'.

Wisdom wrote that it was in Cheltenham that his show business career actually started.

In *Don't Laugh at Me* Norman Wisdom also recalled being on night guard at the Moray House Hotel once a week. *'At 2 a.m., when all was quiet, I would creep round to the back where I had parked my motor bike - next to the Colonel's staff car - and with a length of hose pipe I would quickly siphon out some of his petrol and fill up my small tank to the brim. It would last me the week and the Colonel never suspected.'*

Norman Wisdom, best-known for his 'little man' character in the ill fitting suit and cloth cap, much put upon but struggling through, was awarded a Knighthood in the 2000 Queen's Millennium Honours List for his services to Entertainment. He deliberately tripped as he left the ceremony and the Queen was reported to have been very amused by his antics.

For many years Sir Norman Wisdom joined his former comrades at a dinner at the Carlton Hotel in Cheltenham every September. On his visit on 6 September 2003 he also unveiled the Civic Society plaque commemorating his time in the town with those comrades in the presence of the Mayor and representatives of local theatres and entertainment. The plaque was co-sponsored by the Carlton Hotel. Television cameras recorded highlights of the ceremony and broadcast an interview with Sir Norman. He and the other guests were then entertained by a ladies' barbershop choir before sitting down to satisfy a queue of autograph hunters.

58 and 59 - The Carlton Hotel was redeveloped as the Hotel du Vin and Bistro in 2007. A new plaque, without the earlier hotel name, was erected in 2008.

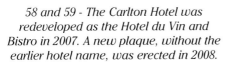

60 - Descendants of Hector Caffieri and Civic Society members at the unveiling of the plaque to the artist in 1986. See p.18.

61 - Magician Paul Daniels and Mayor, Councillor Les Phillips, unveiling the plaque to J.N. Maskelyne, illusionist and watchmaker, in 1989. See p.38.

62 - Esteemed actor Sir Ralph Richardson unveils the plaque at his birthplace in Tivoli Road in 1982. See p.42.

CIVIC SOCIETY
GREEN PLAQUES

PLACES
AND EVENTS

THE CARYATIDS OF MONTPELLIER
Montpellier Walk (map 5 no.31)

Montpellier is a very special part of Cheltenham, but without the Rotunda (at present Lloyds TSB bank) and the caryatids, the 'armless ladies' who support the shop front lintels on their heads, much of its charm would be lost.

The Civic Society responded to a suggestion that the Montpellier caryatids and their carver should be commemorated by a plaque adjacent to

63 - Montpellier Walk

one of them. An original caryatid can be seen in the Cheltenham Art Gallery and Museum and the legend beneath tells her story:

'A caryatid from Montpellier Walk - 1843

'In 1843 a monumental bowed entrance, with shops, was built at the north-end of tree-lined MontpellierWalk, an avenue running from Montpellier Spa, also known as the Rotunda, towards the Promenade.

'The entrance incorporated three terracotta 'caryatids', provided by a London sculptor, Henry Rossi, and loosely based on ancient statues on the Acropolis in Athens.

'Additional caryatids were then carved in stone by a local sculptor, W.G. Brown, and added to the entrance and to the shops that gradually replaced the trees of Montpellier Walk between 1843 and the 1850s.

'This example, one of Rossi's originals, was removed in 1969 so that it could be used as a mould for several new caryatids that were needed for an extension to the bank which then occupied part of the 1843 entrance. It was then given to the Art Gallery and Museum.'

64 - Caryatid

In *A Cheltenham Companion* authors Dr Steven Blake and Aylwin Sampson encourage us to look more closely at each of the caryatids. *'Careful scrutiny of them will reveal that their design is not merely repetitive, for some of them have the right knee forward, others left.'*

The Montpellier Traders' Association co-sponsored the green commemorative plaque that was affixed adjacent to a caryatid to the left of 1 Montpellier Walk. Following the unveiling by the Mayor, Councillor Kenneth Buckland, Dr Steven Blake gave a very informative talk on Montpellier and its history. The Rev. Brian Torode, who had published *The Story of Tivoli* in 1998, stood beside John Henry, Chairman of the Civic Society, at the ceremony on 19 July 2003. It was Brian who had originally suggested that a plaque should commemorate the erection of the caryatids. John Parnett, Chairman of the Montpellier Traders' Association, was also present.

65 - William Giles Brown and his father James working on the Cambray Spa, 1873

Both the plaque and the notice in the Museum record that the caryatids were carved by W.G. Brown of Tivoli. However William Giles Brown, born about 1828, would only have been 15 or 16 at the time.

More recent research by Jill Waller of Cheltenham Local History Society has shown that it was in fact James Brown, William's father, a stone carver of some renown, who won the contract. William and James worked together on the conversion of the Cambray Spa into the Cambray Turkish Baths in 1873, and both worked on the Houses of Parliament. It is reasonable, therefore, to assume that William had been apprenticed to his father at the time that the caryatids were carved.

THE CHELTENHAM ARCHERS
Montpellier Gardens (map 5 no.41)

A Civic Society plaque in Montpellier Gardens commemorates the 150th anniversary of the founding of the Cheltenham Archers in 1857 by Cheltenham solicitor Horace Alfred Ford. Ford, originally from Wales, first picked up a bow in Brighton in 1845 and only four years later he earned his first Champions Medal at the 1849 Grand National meeting in Derby. He won the Championship a total of 12 times from 1849-67. He combined strength, nerve and thoroughness in his revolutionary technique, turning a Victorian amusement into a serious Olympic sport by the application of scientific principles. He is considered by many to be the finest target archer of all time. His book, *Archery: Its Theory and Practice,* published in Cheltenham by Henry Davies in 1856, remains influential today and was republished by Taxus Baccata Books in 2003.

66 - Horace A. Ford scored a total of 1257 at the National Championship in Cheltenham in 1857. His record stood for 72 years

In about 1855 Horace Ford moved to Cheltenham and the following year, perhaps as a result of his influence, the Grand National Archery meeting was held here. He announced his intention to form an archery club in the town and the 26 Cheltenham archers who had shot in the 1856 meeting became the nucleus of the new club. The first meeting of the Cheltenham Archers took place in June 1857 when more than 30 members shot at targets in Montpellier Gardens. Membership was initially limited to 60. The subscription was one guinea, with family membership two guineas.

The Cheltenham Archers met fortnightly in the Gardens under Horace Ford's leadership, and prospered until 1865 when he left Cheltenham to return to South Wales. At that time croquet, another sport considered suitable for women as well as men, became more fashionable and, for a while, membership of the Archers waned. However the Club's fortunes revived after another Grand National Archery meeting was hosted in the town in 1871. The Cheltenham Archers continued to shoot in Montpellier Gardens until 1934 when the Gardens were opened to the general public, and a move became necessary. The membership was reduced to 12 during World War II, but the club has expanded steadily since that time.

The Cheltenham Archers have been exceptionally successful over the past 150 years, winning the Championship Medal 76 times. A Cheltenham Archer has won the Champions Medal every year for over three decades. The Archers can also boast some of the best women archers that the country has ever seen. Alice Blanche Legh was Champion Archer of Great Britain a record-breaking 23 times from 1881-1922, while her sister Beata Mary rarely missed winning a medal in 53 years of national competition from 1885-1938. Cheltenham Archer Queenie Newell became women's champion at the London Olympics in 1908. At the time she won her gold medal she was 53 years and 277 days old. She still holds the record for being the oldest female medallist in the modern Olympics. The Cheltenham Archers have over 100 members today, including several holders of the Champions Medal. The club's ground is now located at Oakleaf Field, Southam.

The green plaque, co-sponsored by the Cheltenham Archers, was unveiled by Mayor, Councillor John Rawson in Montpellier Gardens on 26 April 2008. Mavis Reynolds of the Cheltenham Archers and Civic Society Chairman, John Henry, spoke at the ceremony. Also present was Cheltenham MP Martin Horwood.

67 - The target bosses used by the Cheltenham Archers, illustrated above, were stored under Montpellier bandstand after it was built in 1864. The bosses were probably supplied by John Smith Friskney's sports depot at 23 Pittville Street.

CHELTENHAM CRICKET CLUB
Pavilion, Victoria Cricket Ground, Princes Road
(map 4 no. 23)

68 - Opening of the Victoria Ground pavilion, 21 June 1897

In November 2003 the Chairman of Cheltenham Cricket Club, Peter Simmons, asked the Civic Society if the pavilion on their Victoria Cricket ground at the end of Princes Street would be a suitable site for a Civic Society plaque. It was agreed that a green plaque would commemorate the opening of their first cricket pavilion by Dr W.G. Grace, who played for Gloucestershire Cricket Club from 1870-98. Recognised as the best-known cricketer of his time, Grace is said to have developed many techniques of modern batting.

Cheltenham Cricket Club was formed between 1894-6 on land belonging to Sir James Agg-Gardner, which had previously been market gardens. Dr W.G. Grace officially opened the Victoria Cricket Ground on 21 June 1897, commemorating the occasion of Queen Victoria's Diamond Jubilee the day before. Sir James Agg-Gardner, Cheltenham's Member of Parliament from 1874-80 and on three further occasions, was President and first Life Member of the Club, and a major benefactor for many years. He donated the original pavilion, and in 1907 he paid the balance of a debt which threatened the Club's closure at that time.

69 - Dr W.G. Grace. His family had a long association with cricket in Gloucestershire

As a final act of philanthropy he sold the ground to the Club at a nominal cost in 1920. In 1963 the west end of the ground was sold to finance a new pavilion. Gloucestershire Cricket Club has used the Victoria Ground for first class fixtures over the years, most recently the match between Gloucestershire and the Indian Touring Team in May 1986.

On 21 June 2004 Tom Graveney, local Gloucestershire cricketing hero and President of the MCC from 2004-5, unveiled the green plaque commemorating the opening of the Victoria Grounds, in the presence of the Mayor, Councillor Rob Garnham, and Cheltenham's MP Nigel Jones, both members of the Club. Following the opening speech by John Henry, Chairman of the Civic Society, the other speeches, including that of Tom Graveney, were of a sporting flavour. Inevitably it rained and the cricket match that was to follow had to be cancelled. Some time after this event Cheltenham Cricket Club affixed a small second plaque above the first, which recorded that the Civic Society plaque had been unveiled by Tom Graveney.

Cheltenham has a strong cricketing tradition, and each July the town hosts the world's longest-running cricket festival in the grounds of Cheltenham College. In 1872 James Lilleywhite, popular cricket coach at the College, established a county match there each summer. In August 1878 Lilleywhite was paid £120 to organise two successive county matches on the grounds. 'A pronounced social success', the event became known as Cricket Week. The event was renamed Cheltenham Cricket Festival in 1906 when three county matches were played on the College grounds for the first time. Cheltenham Cricket Festival continues to draw large numbers of visitors to the town to this day.

70 - The first Cricket Club pavilion was situated where the cherry trees are located today

CHELTENHAM GRAMMAR SCHOOL
252-3 High Street (map 1 no.3)

71 - The Victorian Grammar School, High Street. Note the 'dragon and onion' street lamp on the right. Examples of these can still be seen in St Mary's parish churchyard

Most of the shoppers who flock through Wilkinson's store in the High Street will not realise that it is the site of both Cheltenham's original Grammar School and the pseudo-gothic building that replaced it in the 1890s. Some will perhaps remember the Victorian school with its familiar tower, which is shown in relief on the green Civic Society plaque. The all-boys grammar school moved to Princess Elizabeth Way in 1965, and amalgamated with Pate's Grammar School for Girls to form the mixed Pate's Grammar School on the same site in Hester's Way in 1986.

Richard Pate, founder of the Grammar School, was born in Cheltenham in 1516 and after attending the Charity School in the Parish Church he went on to study at Corpus Christi College, Oxford. It was the legal training that he then received at Lincoln's Inn that enabled him to become the Recorder of Gloucester. His experience with the Charity Commissioners led him to see the need for the education of the middle classes. He drew up plans for a *Schola Grammatica* in Cheltenham and the foundation

72 - Richard Pate woodcut portrait

stone was laid in 1572. In 1574 Queen Elizabeth I made a grant of property and land for the endowment of Pate's School and almshouse. Richard Pate died in 1588, having lived to see his school and almshouse firmly established. He was buried in Gloucester Cathedral and his monument now stands in the south transept.

73 - 252-3 High Street

Cheltenham historian, the late John Milner, spent a short while teaching at Cheltenham Grammar School in the High Street. He remembered the cramped conditions at assembly. His geography classroom was at the rear of the building where the ever-pervasive school smells were mixed with the overwhelming smell from the nearby brewery.

Cheltenham Grammar School had six houses from 1922 until their abolition in 1971. One house was called Jessop, after the cricketer Gilbert Jessop and another Baker, after Sir Benjamin Baker, the civil engineer. Both of these famous men are remembered with commemorative plaques in the town; Jessop by a privately-erected bronze plaque in 1975 (see p.101) and Baker by a Civic Society blue plaque in 1985 (see p.14).

Other famous ex-pupils include botanist Sir Rowland Henry Biffen and the composer Gustav Holst. Biffen was born in Cheltenham in 1874, the son of a former headmaster of Christ Church School, Malvern Road. He attended the Grammar School from 1885-92. He became the first Professor of Agricultural Botany at Cambridge in 1908, and is widely regarded as the founder of modern plant genetics. Gustav Holst's association with Cheltenham is celebrated with a Public Libraries Committee plaque on his birthplace at 4 Clarence Road (see p.98).

Robert Kirk, Chairman of Pate's Grammar School Foundation Trustees, co-sponsors, unveiled the Grammar School plaque on 16 March 1993 in the presence of the Mayor, Councillor Brian Cassin.

CHELTENHAM INFANT SCHOOL
St James's Square (map 1 no.2)

74 - *The oldest surviving infant school building in England*
- as it is today

The unassuming stone building by the roundabout on St James's Square is, in fact, a major piece of education history. It is the oldest surviving purpose-built infant school building in England, established by two men who had very strong, and often opposing views on education.

The Rev. Francis Close, charismatic evangelical incumbent of St Mary's Parish Church from 1826-56, had a tremendous influence over the development of education in Victorian Cheltenham. He was involved in the opening of Cheltenham College and was the first President of Cheltenham Ladies' College. His name is even more closely linked with the Anglican Teacher Training College, established on strict 'Scriptural, Evangelical and Protestant principles' which opened in the town in June 1847. The College became St Paul's College for men and St Mary's College for women, and has been the University of Gloucestershire since 2001. Close became Dean of Carlisle after leaving Cheltenham, and following his death his name was given to Dean Close School in Cheltenham.

In 1823 Samuel Wilderspin, an untrained teacher based in London, published *On the Importance of Educating the Infant Poor* in which he wrote that a teacher had to become child-like himself in order to be successful. Having read the book the Rev. Close announced, in his first sermon as incumbent of Cheltenham, that he intended opening an infant school. He invited Samuel Wilderspin to Cheltenham to establish the school in Alstone, then a small hamlet just outside the town. Funds were raised and the small school, one of the earliest in Gloucestershire, opened in Alstone Lane in April 1827 with about 100 pupils. The experiment was a great success and by 1830 the Rev. Close had raised sufficient funds to build a second school in St. James's Square, accommodating about 300 infants.

However Samuel Wilderspin had not been consulted on the second school's construction or staffing, and condemned the fact that it was run largely using the monitorial system, with a curriculum based on the Scriptures and pupils learning by rote. The school flourished, despite the great animosity between the two men, and became an attraction for many visitors to the town. It was one of the first to have playground apparatus, and until recently the remains of the gallery were still visible inside the building. Wilderspin continued his pioneering work in infant education, working from his home at Alpha House, St George's Road until 1839. (see p.100 for details).

75 - The infant school as it was

The co-sponsor of the green Civic Society plaque on St James's Infant School was the College of St Paul and St Mary (see p.57). The plaque was unveiled by the Principal of the College Janet Trotter on 10 October 1987 (see p.107). On 30 October the *Times Educational Supplement* published a photograph of Cheltenham resident, Rosalind Ramirez, a former school inspector, studying the plaque, sheltered by a large umbrella from pouring rain. Rosalind was a Civic Society Committee member for many years and left the Society a small legacy and several prints.

ELECTRICITY SUB-STATION
Corner of Clarence Street and St George's Place
(map 1 no.6)

*76 - The 19th century
Italianate electricity
sub-station*

Cheltenham Local History Society was formed in 1982 and its first *Journal* was published a year later. On the cover was an illustration of the 'Clarence Street Palazzo' by well-known Cheltenham artist and author Aylwin Sampson. The late 19th century electricity sub-station is a prominent feature of Clarence Street. In the *Journal* Roger Beacham described the building as:

'...standing at the junction of St George's Place and that part of Clarence Street formerly known as Manchester Place and being a nineteenth century terracotta building on a rusticated stone plinth... [its] unusual appearance causes a number of enquirers to call at the Public Library close by'.

The red-brick and stone sub-station, originally 2-storeys high, formed part of the town's first electricity supply, and was inaugurated by Cheltenham Borough Council in 1895. The upper floor was added early in the 20th century. Power for the privately-owned electricity supply company was generated by burning rubbish. The sub-station is said to have powered the trams of the Cheltenham & District Light Railway Company that provided public transport in the town from 1901 to 1930.

The building itself was probably designed by Joseph Hall, the Borough Surveyor, who also designed Neptune's Fountain in the Promenade and Cheltenham's distinctive 'dragon and onion' street lamps, as shown in the photograph on p.64. Examples can still be seen in St. Mary's churchyard just a few minutes' walk from the sub-station. The design for the building was based on that of the Strozzi Palace in Florence, which was built in 1489 by one of the wealthiest merchants in the city to imitate and rival the Palazzo Medici.

Cheltenham Civic Society affixed their very first green plaque to the sub-station on 3 May 1986. The co-sponsor of the plaque was the Gloucestershire Society for Industrial Archaeology (GSIA) and the plaque was unveiled by Peter Whittaker, Gloucestershire Divisional General Manager for the Midland Electricity Board, in the presence of the Deputy Mayor, Councillor Don Perry. At the unveiling the Rev. Wilbert Awdry, President of the GSIA, and author of the well-known *Thomas the Tank Engine* children's books, said:'*[The building] is unique. There is no other sub-station in this country which is built in the Italian style.*'

Following various roles spanning both World Wars, the distinctive Italianate sub-station was vacated in 1959 and remained empty for 49 years, despite its Grade II listing. Finally in 2008, the building was re-launched as the 'Strozzi Palace' apartment hotel, following a 12-month, £500,000 conversion, and today advertises six luxurious boutique suites, appropriately fitted out 'in the Italian style'.

77 - Neptune's Fountain on the Promenade, designed by Borough Surveyor Joseph Hall. The River Chelt, which runs below ground here, was probably once the source of water for the fountain, but it is fed by mains water today.

GEORGE III's VISIT IN 1788
Bicentenary Celebrations in 1988

1988 was a very special year for Cheltenham because the town celebrated the bicentenary of the visit of King George III, Queen Charlotte and three royal princesses for five weeks to take the waters from 12 July to 16 August 1788.

The King's presence attracted enormous attention to the town since he rarely ventured outside London. The *Morning Post* reported excitedly that:

'The Cheltenham cap -
the Cheltenham bonnet -
the Cheltenham buttons -
the Cheltenham buckles -
all the fashions are
completely
Cheltenhamised'.

78 - Portrait of George III by Allan Ramsay, 1762

It was this visit that really sparked the development of Cheltenham as the popular destination for visitors that it remains today.

The royal visit was actually made on the recommendation of Sir George Baker, President of the Royal College of Physicians, to treat the King's deteriorating mental and physical health, which was causing serious concern in the summer of 1788. His symptoms are hypothesised by some to have been indicative of the group of blood diseases known as porphyria, and possibly also of arsenic poisoning, which was used to treat the condition.

The royal visitors stayed at Fauconberg Lodge, Bayshill, to which 17 rooms had been added to accommodate them. The quarters were still cramped, especially when the King's son, the Duke of York, joined the party. *The Gentleman's Magazine* reported that, having spotted a neatly-built timber house complete with sash windows at the end of the town, the King suggested that it might be transported to the royal lodgings. Mr Ashton, an ingenious mechanic and surveyor, organised this removal despite having to negotiate a small bridge, and a climb of 50 feet. It took 20 or 30 men six days, much longer than the King had expected, and he prevented them from re-siting the house on the bowling green because it would have spoilt the servants' play. The King paid early morning visits each day to take the waters at the original Old Spa in Bayshill, and at the newer Royal Spa in Overton Road, and spent his days walking around the town and on scenic tours of the area.

A small series of commemorative coins were produced to celebrate George III's visit to Cheltenham. Seven distinct half-guinea and 10 different guinea designs have been identified to date.

A fine commemorative programme was published for Cheltenham's bicentenary celebrations in 1988. The opening article by Dr Steven Blake set the historical scene, and 80 special events were listed, from morris dancing to a searchlight tattoo. Three new Civic Society plaques were also unveiled in the course of the celebrations, at locations of special significance to the royal visit. See p.72. In Pittville Pump Room there was a three-month exhibition covering the Royal visit, and Cheltenham's internationally renowned Festival of Music featured works by Mozart and Haydn, music which the King would have enjoyed. The festivities ended with a spectacular firework display in Pittville Park.

79 and 80 - Obverse and reverse of commemorative George III silvered half-guinea

Fauconberg Lodge - now Sidney Lodge, Overton Road (map 5 no. 27)

To mark the 200th anniversary of King George III's arrival in Cheltenham a green plaque, co-sponsored by Cheltenham Ladies' College, was unveiled on 25 June 1988 at Sidney Lodge, in Overton Road. Now a boarding house for pupils at the College, Sidney Lodge stands on the site of

81 - Sidney Lodge, site of Fauconberg Lodge

Fauconberg Lodge (later known as Bayshill House), where the King and his family stayed during their visit.

The plaque was unveiled by Anthea Jones, Head of the History Department at the Ladies' College. Her *A Short History of the First Cheltenham Spa in Bayshill,* was published by the Ladies' College the same year, as part of the celebrations. The book gives a detailed account of the five-week royal visit, and describes the further development of the Bayshill Estate, including the establishment of the Cheltenham Ladies' College there. The plaque is situated between the two ground floor windows to the left in the photograph above.

Theatre Royal - York Passage, Grosvenor Terrace (map 2 no.13)

A second plaque was unveiled on 2 July 1988 on the site of John Watson's Theatre in York Passage, Grosvenor Terrace, just off the High Street in Cambray. The plaque was co-sponsored by estate agents Reeder and Richards, who owned the premises at that time. King George III visited the theatre three times and it was there that he saw the well-known actress Dorothy Jordan appear as Hippolyta in *She Would and Would Not.* King George's attendance earned the theatre the right to add 'Royal' to its name, and it became known as the Theatre Royal. There is reference to two of the King's visits to the theatre in John Goding's *History of Cheltenham.*

*82 - Site of the
Theatre Royal,
York Passage*

Royal Old Well - now Ladies' College, Bayshill Road (map 5 no.29)

The Duke of Gloucester unveiled a green Civic Society plaque at the main entrance to the Cheltenham Ladies' College on 5 July 1988. The plaque was co-sponsored by the Ladies' College. *'Here'*, the plaque reads, *'was a pathway to the Old Well where King George took the waters in 1788. It was situated near the Princess Hall'*. Chairman David Phillips, Treasurer Don Jones, Sheila Collins and Phil Newcombe of the Civic Society were presented to the Duke on this auspicious occasion.

The main entrance to Cheltenham Ladies' College, on Bayshill Road, was opened by Queen Elizabeth, the Queen Mother, in 1971. The entrance was reconstructed in 1996 and it is thought that the plaque was moved to the right hand side of the entrance steps at about this time.

*83 - The plaque
commemorating King
George III's visit to the Old
Well can now be seen at the
bottom of the steps*

GLOSTER / WHITTLE E28/39
Prototype Jet Aircraft
Former Crabtree Garage, Carlton Street (map 4 no.25)

Frank Whittle's invention of the jet engine was one of the greatest events in aviation history. Both prototypes of the Gloster/Whittle aircraft, powered by his revolutionary engine, were assembled in Cheltenham.

84 -The first E28/39 prototype

Frank Whittle, born in Coventry in 1907, joined the RAF as an Aircraft Apprentice in 1923, but had soon impressed officers with his skills, and in 1926 he was transferred to officer training at RAF Cranwell, a rarity for a 'commoner' at that time. Whittle rose to the rank of Air Commodore but was invalided out in 1948 on the grounds of ill health. He was knighted the same year.

Sir Frank Whittle patented his turbojet engine design in 1929, but it was not until 1936 that work started on the first developmental engine. In September 1939 the Air Ministry contracted the Gloster Aircraft Company (GAC), Hucclecote, to design two prototype aircraft, known as the Gloster/Whittle E28/39, to test Whittle's engine in flight. The first prototype was assembled in Regent Street Garage, now the site of the Regent Arcade. On 15 May 1941 Flight Lieutenant Gerry Sayer successfully flew the aircraft from RAF Cranwell under jet power for the first time. The flight lasted 17 minutes. Dowty's supplied the landing gear for this prototype, and Dowty apprentices crafted the model of this aircraft which is now on display in the Regent Arcade. A glass fibre plaque recording the event was saved when the Regent Street Garage was demolished and when the proposed Jet Age Museum is established it will be re-sited there.

Testing of the second prototype, assembled at Crabtree Garage, Carlton Street, began on 1 March 1943. The aircraft crashed during a test flight on 30 July 1943 after aileron failure caused the controls to jam. The second prototype was destroyed, but the pilot had a miraculous escape.

Experience with the first E28/39 prototype proved invaluable for the development of the Gloster Meteor, Britain's first operational jet fighter aircraft, manufactured by GAC from 1944-54. Today, the first prototype is in the Science Museum, London, alongside the engine, known as the W1, which powered it for the first jet flight in Britain.

85 - Frank Whittle

Frank Whittle paid many visits to Crabtree Garage during assembly of the E28/39 and it is here that the Civic Society green plaque, depicting the aircraft in relief, was unveiled on 25 March 1995 (see p.57). Notables at the ceremony, who had played a major part in the development of the Whittle jet engine, included Lord Kings Norton, Dr C.B.R. Fielden and Dr Geoffrey Bone. The plaque was unveiled by Tony Casson, the Head of Military Business at British Aerospace. James Benn, the retired aeronautical engineer who had originally instigated the erection of the plaque, hosted a reception at his home near Carlton Street after the unveiling.

86 - The old Post Office depot, formerly Crabtree Garage, Carlton Street

The Post Office used the Crabtree Garage as a vehicle depot after World War II. They moved out many years ago and the garage has since been derelict. The Civic Society will re-position the plaque when the site is redeveloped.

GLOUCESTERSHIRE YEOMANRY
First Troop Raised
Entrance to Regent Arcade, High Street (map 2 no.12)

87 - "The Blue Duke". Oil painting by John Chester Mathews,1894. His Grace the Duke of Beaufort reviewing the Royal Gloucestershire Hussars at Prestbury Park

In 1794 British Prime Minister William Pitt, concerned about the possibility of an invasion by Napoleon Bonaparte, proposed that volunteer bodies of cavalry consisting of gentlemen and yeomanry be raised on a county basis under the control of the Lord Lieutenant. Their role was to suppress riots and tumults locally, and for internal defence in the case of invasion from France.

The first such troop of volunteer Gloucestershire Yeomanry was raised by Captain Powell Snell of Guiting Grange at the Plough hotel on 30 July 1795, and this event is recorded on the green Civic Society plaque on the right hand side of the entrance to the Regent Arcade, opposite the plaque that commemorates the Plough itself. Further troops were subsequently raised at Minchinhampton, Wotton-under-Edge, Stow-on-the-Wold, Henbury, Gloucester and Bristol (then part of Gloucestershire). Following the end of the Napoleonic Wars in 1802 all but the Cheltenham Troop were disbanded. War broke out again against the French the following year and 12 troops were raised within the county. Their only action was to quell a riot between Gloucester townsfolk and a detachment of Irish Militia. From 1830 a combination of harsh reforms under the Poor Law, bad harvests, and increased food prices led to unrest amongst agricultural workers. Severe unemployment followed the Land Enclosure Act and the introduction of revolutionary new farming techniques, and rioting began breaking out in the so-called 'Swing' counties in England, including Gloucestershire. Seven troops were raised in the county by landowners to protect their property.

In 1831 Swing riots broke out in Bristol, and were dealt with by troops from Donnington and Tetbury.

In 1834 the Gloucestershire Yeomanry troops amalgamated to form the Gloucestershire Yeomanry Cavalry. Henry Charles Somerset, 6th Duke of Beaufort, was appointed the first commanding officer, and the Beaufort family continued to have strong associations with the regiment over many years. The title 'Royal' was graciously granted by Queen Victoria in 1841 and in 1847 the Regiment was restyled the Royal Gloucestershire Hussars as part of a wider reorganisation of the English army. Amusingly moustaches were declared to be compulsory within the regiment in 1846, and an edict at that time stated that 'where it is impossible to grow the article substitutes may be supplied from the barbers'.

The Royal Gloucestershire Hussars have had a very distinguished war record. The regiment first saw active service in the Boer War and suffered heavy casualties in the trenches at Gallipoli in World War I. They switched from horses to tanks in 1922 and fought as Desert Rats in North Africa in World War II from 1941, again sustaining severe losses. In 1947 the regiment became part of the newly-formed Territorial Army.

The unveiling of the green Civic Society plaque to commemorate the formation of the Gloucestershire Yeomanry in 1795 took place on 12 September 1997. It was a colourful occasion. Lieutenant-Colonel David Ashford-Sandford pulled away the curtain on the plaque, in the presence of the Mayor, Councillor Les Godwin, and a uniformed Hussar (see p.90). The plaque bears the Hussars' cap badge in relief.

88 - Royal Gloucestershire Hussars' Summer Camp at the race course, Prestbury Park 1914

MONTPELLIER BANDSTAND
Montpellier Gardens (map 5 no.40)

89 - The refurbished bandstand & proscenium in the summer of 2007

Montpellier Gardens have always been a fashionable venue for public entertainment in the town. The Gardens were laid out in 1831 as a pleasure ground for visitors to Montpellier Spa which opened in 1809. The original spa building was replaced by the Rotunda in 1817 (now Lloyds TSB bank) and the dome was added in 1825. The Gardens passed into municipal ownership in the early 20th century. The Victorian bandstand in Montpellier Gardens is one of only two to have survived in the town. It was constructed in 1864 to a design by the Coalbrookdale Company, Ironbridge. A second, much smaller example, constructed of wood and shingle, can be seen near Pittville Pump Room. Another cast-iron example once stood in Imperial Gardens, but sadly was sold to Bognor Regis in 1948 for £175. The Gustav Holst Memorial Fountain has now been erected on this site (see p.122). A fourth bandstand stood beside Pittville Park boating lake.

The Montpellier Gardens bandstand was rescued from dereliction and restored by the Civic Society, and was reopened by Sir Charles Irving MP on 20 July 1994. Mayor, Councillor Deborah Griggs, also attended the ceremony. A green Civic Society plaque commemorates the event, and the fact that it is the oldest bandstand in the country still in regular use. In June 2004 Cheltenham Borough Council was awarded £722,000 by the Heritage Lottery Fund and in July 2004 the Friends of Montpellier Bandstand and Gardens displayed the plans for the £1.25 million development of the Gardens. The complete restoration of many 1923 features was completed in 2007, and included renovation of the distinctive proscenium, built in the early 20th century, which is now The Gardens Gallery, a community art gallery for local artists and other arts-related activities. The bandstand was redecorated for the official reopening of Montpellier Gardens on 9 July 2007.

PARACHUTE DESCENT
First successful descent by an Englishman
Montpellier Gardens (map 5 no.39)

90 - John Hampton's ascent and descent,
as seen from Montpellier Gardens

On 3 October 1838 John Hampton (b.1799) became the first Englishman to make a successful parachute drop, when he descended from his gas-filled balloon which had risen from Montpellier Gardens, opposite the Montpellier Spa Pump Room (now Lloyds Bank).

No event in fashionable locations such as Vauxhall Gardens, London, and Cheltenham, was considered complete without a balloon ascent in the early 19th century, and Cheltenham played host to some of the greatest aeronauts of the day. The most famous was Charles Green, who made balloon flights from Cheltenham in 1822 and 1837, and who completed more than 500 ascents in total between 1821 and his retirement in 1852. Competition between aeronauts was fierce, and in September 1838 John Hampton announced dramatically that he intended making a daring parachute descent from his Albion balloon in Montpellier Gardens, Cheltenham.

Both the ancient Chinese and Leonardo da Vinci are credited with the idea of the parachute, and in 1797 Frenchman Andre Garnerin successfully put the idea into practice. Garnerin made a successful drop in London in 1802, but there were no further attempts in England until 24 July 1837 when Robert Cocking, an English amateur scientist, attempted a descent from Charles Green's enormous Nassau balloon. Cocking and parachute weighed nearly 400lb in total and his descent, almost inevitably, proved fatal and nearly cost the lives of the vastly-experienced Green and co-pilot. The tragedy strengthened the view in England that such stunts merely pandered to morbid public curiosity.

For two days before his planned descent John Hampton exhibited his 'improved safety parachute' in Montpellier Pump Room. The parachute was umbrella-shaped, 15 feet in diameter, made of canvas, whalebone and bamboo, and weighed about 200 lb. Cheltenham magistrates only allowed Hampton access to the town's gas supply if he tethered the balloon. However, on reaching 300 feet, Hampton severed the restraining ropes and at about 9,000 feet he cut loose his parachute. Spectators watched in horror as the gas-filled balloon exploded, but Hampton escaped, jettisoning 56lb of ballast before landing safely at Badgeworth just over 12 minutes later. John Hampton went on to make six further parachute descents, and had completed a total of over 100 flights in his *Albion* and *Erin-go-bragh* balloons by the time he retired in 1852.

A Civic Society plaque was unveiled on the bandstand in Montpellier Gardens on 3 Oct 2008, celebrating Hampton's descent exactly 170 years earlier. The plaque, co-sponsored by the British Parachute Association, was unveiled by Andy Scott (who comes from Cheltenham) and Paul Applegate, both from the Association. Also at the ceremony were Civic Society Chairman John Henry; Martin Horwood MP; Mayor, Councillor Robin MacDonald, five members of the Silver Stars Parachute Team from the Royal Logistics Corps based in South Cerney, and an enthusiastic crowd of onlookers.

91 - A spectacular display by the Silver Stars Parachute Team, launched the plaque-unveiling ceremony

PLOUGH HOTEL
Entrance to Regent Arcade, High Street (map 2 no.11)

92 - The 1980s façade of the Regent Arcade echoes that of The Plough

Few visitors to Cheltenham entering the Regent Arcade realise that The Plough, the town's leading hotel, once stood there. One painting of The Plough in Cheltenham Art Gallery and Museum, dated about 1740, shows the original coaching inn with stepping stones across a muddy street. Another painting in the museum, dated 1870, entitled *Changing Horses at the Plough* shows a much grander building. In the coaching days it had stables for 100 horses.

The Plough played an important part in the history of the town and had many notable visitors. The Grand Duke Nicholas stayed there in 1816, and the Duke of Cambridge in 1835. The violin virtuoso Paganini also stopped there in 1831. After two successful concerts at the nearby Assembly Rooms he ran into some trouble when he refused to give an extra performance at the Theatre Royal.

In addition to The Plough's importance as a coaching inn, much of the town's business was conducted there, and it was the ideal venue for protests, presentations and celebrations. The business of the Cotswold Hunt took place there and in 1851 a meeting was held to establish the Stag Hounds. Baron de Ferrières held a banquet there in honour of W.G. Grace and his eleven during the first Cheltenham Cricket Week in 1877. It is interesting to note that back in 1772 John Wesley, founder of the Methodist movement, preached from the old Market House opposite the hotel.

The importance of The Plough to life in Cheltenham can be demonstrated by the fact that George Rowe selected the building as the starting point for his first walk around the town in his *Illustrated Cheltenham Guide,* first published in 1845. Rowe says:

'We proposed making the Plough Hotel our starting point, because of its conveniently central situation, and also because that it has ever been identified with the early history of Cheltenham; from the humble inn it has risen through successive stages of development , keeping pace with the onward progress of the town itself. ...The present proprietor Mr J.B. Churchill, has spared no expense to make the House efficient in every department, and his exertions have earned [the Hotel] a name as well known as was the Southwark Tabard ... so graphically described by the immortal Chaucer.'

The Plough was demolished in 1983 and the Regent Arcade was erected in its place. To the left of the High Street entrance to the Arcade is the green Civic Society commemorative plaque, with an illustration of the old hotel in relief. The plaque was unveiled on 23 May 1997 by the Mayor, Councillor Les Godwin, attended by Robert Wilson, Chairman of the Civic Society. At the time of writing (2008) there are plans to remodel the High Street entrance to the Arcade.

93 and 94 - The Plough hotel (above). An artist's impression (right) of the proposed new High Street entrance to the Regent Arcade, which was displayed in the Arcade, Sept 2008

RECORD TEMPERATURE
Montpellier Gardens (map 5 no.38)

95 - Meteorological Station, Montpellier Gardens, prior to its removal in 2001

Many Cheltenham residents will remember the meteorological station in Montpellier Gardens. Frank Ford lived at the lodge in the Gardens, and took five readings at station no. 4967 every day for 33 years, until he retired in March 2001. Before coming to Cheltenham he had been a meteorological officer in Birmingham for 10 years. On 3 August 1990 Frank Ford took a reading of 37.1 degrees Centigrade (98.8 degrees Fahrenheit). At that time, it was the highest temperature ever recorded in Great Britain. A small bronze plaque was placed behind the station to commemorate this record. The equipment was removed from the Gardens in 2001 and the official meteorological thermometer was moved to Gloucestershire Airport, Staverton. Thought to have been lost in 2001, the plaque was subsequently rediscovered, and affixed to the refreshment kiosk in the Gardens.

In August 2003 Cheltenham lost its 13-year record to Gravesend, Kent, when a temperature of 38.1 degrees Centigrade (100.6 degrees Fahrenheit) was recorded there. Nevertheless the Friends of Montpellier Bandstand and Gardens wished to commemorate Cheltenham's record. They co-sponsored the Civic Society plaque, which was also fixed to the refreshment kiosk, and which was unveiled by Frank Ford on 24 July 2004. The Cheltenham Brass Band played in the Montpellier bandstand (see p.78), adding greatly to the happy occasion on a lovely day.

96 - Montpellier Gardens refreshment kiosk

RUGBY LEAGUE CENTENARY
FIRST INTERNATIONAL TOUR
St John's Avenue, opposite Bence's entrance
(map 4 no.19)

97 - Location of the rugby league plaque

The part of Cheltenham's Inner Ring Road, known as St John's Avenue, may seem an unlikely setting for one of the most significant sporting events of the early 20th century. However it was here that the Cheltenham Athletic Ground grandstand stood until 1982, and it was at the Athletic Ground that the deciding game of the very first international rugby league tour took place between England and New Zealand on 15 Feb 1908.

Rugby is traditionally said to have started at Rugby School, Warwickshire in 1823 and the game, later known as rugby union, quickly spread throughout England and Wales. However the declared amateur status of the game caused financial difficulties for working class players, particularly in Wales and the north, who were forced to take time off work in order to be able to play. On 29 August 1895 21 English clubs voted to form a separate group, known as the Northern Union, in which players were '*allowed compensation for bona fide loss of time*'. The new game had 13 players rather than 15 per team, was faster and had fewer stoppages in play. Rugby league, as it became known, grew rapidly in popularity and by 1897 there were 80 clubs across the country. In 1898 professionalism was fully adopted by the Northern Union.

98 - Flyer for the historic game in Cheltenham

- 84 -

New Zealand already had a national rugby union team, the All Blacks, but in 1906 Albert Henry Baskerville, a Wellington postal clerk and one of the country's top rugby union players, masterminded the first international rugby league tour to England, Wales and Australia. The team, disparagingly dubbed the 'All Golds' because of the 'serpent of professionalism', was made up of All Blacks and provincial players, some of whom had never played rugby league before. The team arrived at Folkestone on 30 September, after a voyage lasting over a month. Each player had contributed £50 to the tour fund and paid themselves £1 per day from the time of their arrival in England. Their country-wide tour schedule over the following five months was punishing, with 25 games against clubs, three against county sides and two against the Welsh and English XIIIs.

The highlights of the tour were the three international games between the All Golds and the Northern Union sides. On 25 January New Zealand lost the first game 14-16 at Headingley, but then won 18-6 at Chelsea on 8 February. Cheltenham had probably been selected for the deciding final game because the first-ever All Blacks rugby union touring team had played there in 1905-6. It therefore

99 - Albert Baskerville

provided an important showcase for rugby league in what was still very much a rugby union stronghold. Despite heavy rain the All Golds won the third game 8-5 at Cheltenham on 15 February, thereby winning the British leg of the tour. The New Zealanders returned home via Australia, playing several games there in early May. Tragically Albert Baskerville, who had provided the inspiration and drive for the whole tour, died of influenza and pneumonia in Brisbane on 20 May 1908, aged only 25.

Kevin Nicholas, Rugby Football League President, and Brad Tindall, representing the New Zealand Rugby League, unveiled the Civic Society plaque on 15 Feb 2008. Other guests included MP Martin Horwood; Mayor, Councillor John Rawson, and John Henry, Civic Society Chairman. Tony Collins, Professor of Social History of Sport at Carnegie University, said that 'the Kiwis adventure was unparalleled in sport'. The game's centenary was celebrated throughout 2008, and included the first Cheltenham Rugby Festival on 3-4 May when league teams competed for the All Golds and 1908 Cups.

ST JAMES'S STATION
Waitrose Superstore, Honeybourne Way
(map 6 no.44)

100 - View across the site of St James's Station towards Waitrose from the foot and cycle bridge

Looking at the Cheltenham Waitrose site, which extends from Gloucester Road to St Georges Road, with the landscaped River Chelt and the white Sydney Harbour-like foot and cycle bridge, it is hard to imagine that this was once railway ground, and before that part of Jessop's Nursery and gardens, described in *Rowe's Illustrated Cheltenham Guide* as *'one of the most pleasing spots in the locality of Cheltenham'.* See p.87.

In 1836 the Cheltenham and Great Western Act authorised a railway line to Swindon via Gloucester, Stonehouse, Stroud and Kemble, but it was not until 1847 that the first Great Western Railway (GWR) station was opened with a broad gauge track from Gloucester. The station, a poor affair, was sited at the end of Knapps Lane, near to where St Gregory's Primary School is located today. The track was converted to standard gauge in 1872, and later the station was rebuilt with an imposing *porte-cochère* entrance on St James's Square, allowing passengers to alight from their carriages under cover. See p.89.

101 - Many visitors came to admire exotic plants, such as rice, bananas and breadfruit which grew in Jessop's Nursery. Advertisement in Griffith's Historic Description of Cheltenham (1826)

102 - St James's Station with the towers of St Gregory's (right) and St Matthew's churches in background

103 - The 'Cheltenham Flyer' with a full head of steam

The most famous train to pull into St. James's Station on a regular basis was the 'Cheltenham Spa Express' which ran from Cheltenham to London. In 1923 the Express, known affectionately as the 'Cheltenham Flyer', held the British railway's speed record on the run from Swindon to Paddington at 61.8mph. In 1929 it achieved a world speed record. Beaten by the Canadians, it took the record again a year later. After World War II the train became just another London express. Sadly St James's Station closed on 1 January 1966. The frontage to St James's Square was developed immediately, but the extensive site behind remained a wasteland until the building of the Waitrose store and garage in 2002.

104 - The gates at St James's Place, Jessop Avenue, celebrate the 'Cheltenham Flyer'

It was in response to a request from the Gloucestershire Society for Industrial Archaeology (GSIA) that the green Civic Society plaque commemorating both GWR stations was erected on the main entrance to Waitrose on Honeybourne Way. The site chosen for the plaque is the location of the first station, for which no illustrations are known to exist. The building depicted on the plaque itself is the second station, which was on the site of the office block fronting St. James's Square. The plaque was unveiled on 2 April 2003 by the Mayor, Councillor Kenneth Buckland. Amina Chatwin, President of the GSIA, gave a delightful and nostalgic speech to conclude the ceremony.

105 - The imposing porte-cochère to the second St. James's Station, as depicted on the plaque

107 - Unveiling the plaque
on the oldest surviving
infant school building in
the country. See p.66.

106 - Phil Newcombe
and a member of the
Gloucestershire
Hussars in splendid full
dress uniform at the
unveiling of the
Yeomanry plaque at
the Regent Arcade.
See p.76.

108 - Tom Graveney
unveiling the plaque at
Cheltenham Cricket Club
in 2004. See p.62.
Graveney played for
England in 79 Tests, and
captained the national
team in 1968.His
unveiling of the pavilion
plaque is
commemorated with a
small plaque above this
one.

OTHER
PLAQUES

ADAM LINDSAY
GORDON
1833 — 1870
THE POET OF
AUSTRALIA
LIVED HERE
IN BOYHOOD

CHARLES STURT
AUSTRALIAN EXPLORER
LIVED HERE
1863 - 1869

GUSTAV HOLST
COMPOSER
WAS BORN HERE
21st. SEPT. 1874

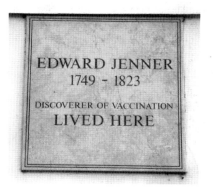

EDWARD JENNER
1749 - 1823
DISCOVERER OF VACCINATION
LIVED HERE

FRED ARCHER (1857-86)
Champion Jockey
St George's Cottage, 43 St George's Place (map 1 no.5)

109 - Fred Archer and his daughter Nellie Rose shortly before his tragic death in 1886

Victorian champion jockey Frederick James Archer was born at St George's Cottage, St George's Place in Cheltenham on 11 January 1857. Fred grew up in Prestbury where his father William, a steeplechase rider who had won the Grand National on *Little Charley* in 1858, had retired to become landlord of the King's Arms, taking over from his father-in-law. It has been claimed that Fred Archer is England's most famous jockey.

At the age of 11 Fred Archer was apprenticed for five years to top trainer Mathew 'Mat' Dawson following advice from Richard de Sales La Terrière of the Cotswold Hunt. Fred rode his first winner in a steeplechase at Bangor, Wales, aged just 12 and weighing only 4st 11lb. He boasted a remarkable record by the end of his life - 2,148 winners from 8,004 rides from 1869-86. During this period he was champion jockey of England for 13 consecutive years from 1874-86. In total he won 25 classic races, including the Epsom Derby five times in 1877, 1880-1 and 1885-6. At the peak of his career he was said to have been worth half a million pounds.

Fred Archer maintained his links with Cheltenham, spending weeks with his family in Prestbury and continuing to ride with the Cotswold Hunt. His friends included Cheltenham solicitor Charles Jessop.

At 5ft 8½in Fred Archer was tall for a jockey, and he had to diet and take purgatives constantly to keep his weight under control. This had an adverse effect on his health. He ran into debt and sank into severe depression following the death of his newborn son William in January 1884, and of his wife Helen shortly after giving birth to their daughter Nellie Rose on 7 November the same year. He sank further into despair when he contracted typhoid, and tragically committed suicide by shooting himself on 8 November 1886 at his stables in Newmarket. He was only 29. Archer is buried with his wife and son in Newmarket cemetery. Since his death at his stables, now known as the Pegasus Stables, there have been many reported sightings of Archer on a ghostly white horse. Archer's daughter Nellie was brought up by her maternal grandparents, John Dawson, a race-horse trainer, and his wife Ada in Newmarket.

A plaque on St George's Cottage, 43 (formerly no. 52) St George's Place commemorates Fred Archer's birthplace. An earlier plaque had been incorrectly located on no. 53, the cottage facing St George's Place, instead of the cottage behind. On removal this first plaque was lost and Mrs M. Pratley, who owned St George's Cottage in 1971, paid for a replacement to be erected on the correct location in the autumn of that year. It is not possible to see the plaque from St George's Place, but it may be viewed on application by letter to the present owner.

Cheltenham author Edith M. Humphris published the first full-length biography of Archer in 1923 called *The Life of Fred Archer*. She also published *The Life of Mathew Dawson,* about Fred's mentor, in 1928.

Dr Steven Blake, formerly of Cheltenham Art Gallery and Museum, organised an exhibition of Fred Archer's life at Pittville Pump Room between November 1986 and January 1987. A comprehensive catalogue, written by Steven Blake, accompanied the exhibition.

110 - The commemorative plaque at St George's Cottage

DR THOMAS COLLEDGE (1796-1879)
Pioneering Eye Surgeon
Lauriston House, Montpellier Street (map 5 no.35)

111 - Detail of portrait of Dr Thomas Colledge painted by George Chinnery in Macau 1830-40

Pioneering eye surgeon Dr Thomas Richardson Colledge lived in Cheltenham for the last 38 years of his life, the last 30 of which were at Lauriston House, Montpellier Street. He died at the house on 28 October 1879, aged 82.

Thomas Colledge studied medicine under Sir Astley Cooper, an old friend of Dr Edward Jenner. After qualifying as a surgeon at Leicester Infirmary he joined the East India Company in China in 1819. Soon afterwards he was transferred to the service of the Crown, becoming Superintendent-Surgeon of hospitals in Canton, Macao and Whampoa. In 1827 Colledge set up an Ophthalmic Infirmary in Macao. In the 1830s pioneering medical missionaries in China, such as Colledge, argued that: '... *medical practice among the Chinese [could] bring about a more social and friendly intercourse between them and foreigners*'. Medical missionaries often favoured the practice of eye surgery because it could produce the dramatic effect of restoring the vision, and had the religious connotation of making a blind person see. Colledge became a founder member and Chairman of the Medical Missionary Society (MMS), established on 21 February 1838. The object of the Society was to assist medical missionaries on arrival in China.

On his return from the Far East Dr Thomas Colledge became a consulting physician in Cheltenham in 1839. He may have been drawn to the town because it was considered to be a great medical centre, and many of the pioneers of Jenner's day were still in practice. He became a busy and valued practitioner in the town for 38 years. During this time he received many national professional honours - including being made President of the Medical Missionary Society for life.

In October 1861, more than 20 years after his arrival and after years of planning, Dr Colledge formally opened the Cheltenham Ophthalmic Infirmary at Bournemouth House (now no. 11), St George's Place, with himself as consulting physician and Walter Hamilton Jessop as consulting surgeon. It was the very earliest days of eye surgery and for the 206 cases that were dealt with in the first five months their work must have seemed miraculous. The institution developed a national reputation within its first year.

In 1976 the owners of the restored Lauriston House, Montpellier, unveiled a plaque commemorating the residence there of Dr Thomas Colledge.

112 and 113 - Lauriston House, Montpellier. The plaque is situated underneath the lower window to the right of the porch.

ADAM LINDSAY GORDON (1833-70)
Poet & Champion Jockey
Court House, 28 Priory Street (map 4 no.20)

114 - Adam Lindsay Gordon c.1862

Poet Adam Lindsay Gordon, considered by many to be the National Poet of Australia, was born in the Azores in 1833, where his mother's father had a plantation. He attended Cheltenham College in 1841 as one of its first pupils, when his father, formerly a Captain in the Bengal Cavalry, became the Hindustani master there. The family lived in a large Regency town house called Court House at 28 Priory Street (formerly no.25).

Gordon was a wild boy, and spent much of his time steeple-chasing and bare-knuckle boxing. Cheltenham-born boxing legend Jem Edwards, one-time national lightweight champion and landlord of the Roebuck Inn, Lower High Street, coached Cheltenham College boys including Gordon in the art. On one famous occasion Gordon knocked Edwards out by a fluke. Gordon was sent to the Royal Military College, Woolwich but got into trouble there and was asked to leave. He returned to Cheltenham College for a short while in 1851, but completed his education at the Royal Grammar School, Worcester from 1851 onwards, despite nearly being imprisoned for stealing a horse to ride in the Worcester Steeplechase.

In despair at his son's behaviour Gordon's father sent him to Australia in 1853, where he enlisted in the mounted police. Two years later, when he was a travelling horse-breaker and trainer, he met a Roman Catholic missionary and naturalist, who encouraged Gordon in his poetry writing. He became an MP for South Australia in 1864 and achieved national celebrity as a jockey. However his life was fraught with difficulties. He suffered a severe head injury in a riding accident, was bankrupted by a fire in the livery stable, ran into debt, drank, gambled and borrowed heavily into pursue a court case that he eventually lost, and mourned the death of his infant daughter Annie, aged only 11 months.

Gordon made his living as a steeple-chase jockey and a writer, publishing several volumes of poetry. The last was published on 24 June 1870. Tragically, the following day, burdened with money worries, he committed suicide on Brighton Beach, Melbourne. The book, called *Bush Ballads and Galloping Rhymes,* is now regarded as one of the most important pieces of Australian literature. The collection included a poem called *How We Beat the Favourite*, which is said to have been written about the steeplechase at Cheltenham in 1847.

In May 1934 a bust of Adam Lindsay Gordon was placed in Poets' Corner, Westminster Abbey in London. He is the only Australian poet to have been honoured in this way. A festival celebrating Gordon's life and work was first held in Melbourne in 2006 and now takes place annually on the anniversary of the poet's death. The name of the festival - National Froth and Bubble Day - is a line from his poem *Ye Wearie Wayfarer,* published in 1865-6:

Life is full of froth and bubble
Two things stand like stone
Kindness in another's trouble
Courage in your own.

The plaque to Adam Lindsay Gordon was unveiled at his boyhood home, 28 Priory Street, Cheltenham, by the writer Douglas Brooke Wheelton Sladen on 19 October 1933 (see p.91). Sladen published *Adam Lindsay Gordon and His Friends in England and Australia* in 1912, co-written with local Cheltenham author Edith M. Humphris.

115 - Court House,
28 Priory Street

GUSTAV HOLST (1874-1934)
Composer
4 Clarence Road (map 3 no.17)

One of Cheltenham's most distinguished sons must surely be Gustavus Theodor von Holst, better known as composer Gustav Holst.

116 - Gustav Holst

Holst, was born to a family of Swedish descent on 21 September 1874 at 4 Clarence Road. He attended Cheltenham Grammar School, where his father Adolph taught music, from the summer of 1887 until Christmas the following year. Holst was a bright boy, excelling in English, Divinity, French and German, but he did not enjoy his time at the school. He suffered from severe asthma and was often so weak after an attack that he could barely crawl upstairs to bed. He did not play sports at school because of his health and was consequently teased by his fellow pupils.

117 - Lansdown Castle, built as a house in the 1850s, became a grocer's and a tobacconist's. Demolished c.1972

Gustav Holst's father Adolph was an accomplished pianist, who gave recitals at the Assembly Rooms and was organist at All Saints' Church, Pittville. His grandfather was a well-known harp teacher and his mother, who died when he was eight, was a singer. Holst also showed an early aptitude for music and began composing at the age of 12. In 1892 Gustav Holst wrote an operetta entitled *Lansdown Castle*, named after a crenellated building at the junction of Lansdown

Road and Gloucester Road. The piece was enthusiastically received when it was performed at Cheltenham Corn Exchange. Adolph Holst borrowed money to send his son to the Royal College of Music, London in 1893 and it was there that Holst became friends with Gloucestershire-born composer Ralph Vaughan Williams. Despite his poor health Holst often walked or cycled much of the way home from the College.

118 - Holst with Mayor of Cheltenham, 1927

Holst composed many hundreds of works, and wrote in a wide variety of musical styles, from songs for solo voice and chamber music to opera and full orchestral works. He drew inspiration from many sources, including Sanskrit and English folk songs. In 1927 Cheltenham hosted a Holst Festival to honour one of the town's best-known sons and, despite ill health, Holst himself conducted the Birmingham Orchestra performance of *The Planets,* his best-known work. He died on 25 May 1934 aged 59 and his ashes are interred in Chichester Cathedral.

119 - The Holst Birthplace Museum

The Holst Birthplace Museum was opened on 21 October 1975 by the Duke of Beaufort. The story of the man and his music is told through a fascinating display of his personal belongings. The museum, a fine Regency house, shows the upstairs-downstairs way of life, and includes a working Victorian kitchen and laundry, and charming Edwardian nursery. The white ceramic plaque, affixed by the Public Libraries Committee, was unveiled by Sir Ralph Vaughan Williams on 30 June 1949 (see p.91). The Civic Society statue to Holst, erected in 2008, can be seen in Imperial Gardens (see p.114).

DR EDWARD JENNER (1749-1823)
Pioneer of Vaccination
Alpha House, St George's Road (map 6 no.45)

120 - Alpha House, base for Jenner's vaccination programme, and centre for Wilderspin's infant education innovation

A Public Library Tablets Sub-Committee plaque to Dr Edward Jenner was unveiled at Alpha House, St George's Road by the Mayor, Councillor H.T. Bush, on 17 May 1949 (see p.91). The plaque recorded that 'Edward Jenner discoverer of vaccination lived here'. The old farmhouse was certainly significant as the base for Jenner's ground-breaking work, vaccinating the poor of Cheltenham against smallpox; in 1809 Jenner claimed that he had successfully vaccinated 3-4,000 people in the Cheltenham area during one epidemic. Local historian Jill Waller has recently proved that Alpha House belonged to surgeon Thomas Cother during this time, and that Jenner was actually living in St George's Place rather than at Alpha House (see p.32).

Alpha House has another significant claim to fame. Samuel Wilderspin, pioneering advocate of infant education, came to Cheltenham in the 1820s to help set up an infant school in Alstone at the instigation of the Rev. Francis Close. However the men argued vehemently over educational methods at a second infant school in St James's in 1830 (see p.66). Wilderspin lived in Alpha House at that time and defiantly set up an Infant School Depot there, lecturing on infant education across Britain, and supplying his newly-founded schools with books and equipment from the house. Wilderspin's association with Cheltenham ended in 1839 when he moved to Dublin, but his influence continued, and by 1846 there were five infant schools in the town.

GILBERT LAIRD JESSOP (1874-1955)
Cricketer
30 Cambray Place (map 2 no.9)

Gilbert Laird Jessop, considered by many to have been the greatest hitter in the history of cricket, was born at 30 Cambray Place, Cheltenham on 19 May 1874.

Jessop, the son of a Cheltenham surgeon who was also a Governor of the Pate's Foundation, attended Cheltenham Grammar School from 1885-9. He had to leave school at 15, following the early death of his father, but by then he had already played for the School's 1st XI, at the tender age of 12. He worked as an apprentice schoolmaster before financing his own admission to Cambridge, where he became Captain of the University Cricket Club in 1899.

121 - Gilbert Laird Jessop

Jessop first played for Gloucestershire County Cricket Club in 1894. He captained the side from 1898-1913, taking over from W.G. Grace, who had led the team for 28 years. He won his first Test cap in 1899, and played in a total of 18 Tests. He scored 104 against the Australians at the Oval in 1902, saving the match for England. An all-rounder, and nicknamed 'The Croucher', he was an excellent wicket-keeper and an aggressive batsman. He scored a double century in two hours in 1903 - when sixes were unrecognised - and once scored a century in 40 minutes. In total he scored 53 first class centuries, averaging 82.7 runs per hour throughout his career.

The bronze commemorative plaque erected on Gilbert Jessop's birthplace at 30 Cambray Place was provided by Gerald Brodribb, author of *The Legend of Gilbert Jessop,* published in 1974. The plaque was unveiled by Gilbert Jessop's son, the Rev. Gilbert Jessop on 4 August 1975.

WILLIAM CHARLES MACREADY (1793-1873)
Actor
6 Wellington Square (map 3 no. 14)

122 - William Macready

Celebrated Shakespearean actor William Charles Macready retired to 6 Wellington Square, Cheltenham in 1860, and lived at this address until his death in 1873.

Macready made his stage debut in 1810 as Romeo in Birmingham at a theatre managed by his father. After the death of Edmund Kean in 1833 Macready became the leading actor of his time. He managed Covent Garden from 1837-9 and the Drury Lane Theatre from 1841-3, and made several successful tours to the USA. His last US visit in 1849 was marred by a riot at the Astor Opera House, New York incited by an envious American actor Edwin Forrest. The riot led to the death of seventeen people, shot by the military called out to quell the disturbance.

Macready gave his farewell performance as Macbeth at Drury Lane on 26 February 1851. After retiring to Cheltenham he lectured and read aloud in the town, and his friend Charles Dickens is known to have stayed with him on several occasions in the 1860s, whilst doing reading tours of provincial theatres. Macready died in Cheltenham on 27 April 1873.

The bronze plaque to William Charles Macready was erected at 6 Wellington Square by the Public Libraries Committee and was unveiled by his son, Sir Neville Macready, on 15 March 1927.

123 - 6 Wellington Square

JOHN NEVIL MASKELYNE (1839-1917)
Illusionist and Watchmaker
Everyman Theatre, Regent Street (map 2 no.7)

On 7 May 1947 Noel Maskelyne unveiled a brass plaque at the Old Town Hall, Regent Street commemorating the site on which his grandfather, Cheltenham-born Victorian illusionist John Nevil Maskelyne, had witnessed the magical séance by American spiritualists, the Davenport Brothers. The plaque was sponsored by the Cotswold Magical Society.

124 - The first Maskelyne plaque

The Maskelyne plaque was removed from the Old Town Hall when the building was demolished to make way for the Regent Arcade in 1983-4, and for many years its whereabouts were unknown. Then in 2002 Dougie Gibbard, a Cotswold Magical Society committee member, located the plaque and in 2005 it was re-sited inside the foyer of the Everyman Theatre, just a short distance from its original location. The plaque was unveiled by Alan Shaxon, President of the Magic Circle, on 6 June 2005. Alan wore his official badge of office, which includes the names of Maskelyne's son Nevil, who was born in Cheltenham, and grandson Clive, both of whom had also held the office of President.

125 - Alan Shaxon unveils the first plaque in its new location at the Everyman Theatre

A blue Civic Society plaque is located on 12 Rotunda Terrace, Montpellier, Maskelyne's home from about 1860-73. See p.38 for details of the second plaque, and more about Maskelyne and his exposure of the fraudulent Davenport Brothers.

CHARLES STURT (1795-1869)
Explorer of Australia
19 Clarence Square (map 3 no.15)

The 19th century explorer Charles Sturt retired to Cheltenham in 1853 and spent the last six years of his life living at 19 Clarence Square.

126 - Charles Sturt c.1849

Sturt, who was born in India, took an army commission in 1813, seeing action with the Duke of Wellington in Spain and at Waterloo. He served elsewhere in Europe and in Canada until 1826. He rose to the rank of Captain in the 39th Regiment of Foot and, with his regiment, he escorted convicts to New South Wales, arriving in Australia in 1827. The same year he was appointed Military Secretary to Sir Ralph Darling, Governor of New South Wales. Between 1828-44 Sturt, a born leader, enthusiastic botanist and talented writer and artist, led a number of expeditions into the unexplored interior of Australia. He and his teams rowed 2,000 miles in order to plot the rivers between Sydney and Adelaide, and discovered and named the Murray and Darling rivers.

In Australia Sturt is still remembered for his courage and endurance, and his achievements earned him the name of 'Father of Australian Discovery'. Sturt Stony Desert, the Sturt River and Sturt's Desert Pea are named after him and New South Wales honoured him with the Charles Sturt University. The Public Libraries Committee's plaque on Charles Sturt's retirement home at 19 Clarence Square was unveiled by Mr. J.A. Beasley, Australian High Commissioner, on 16 June 1948. See plaque on p.91. A water bottle used by the explorer was presented to the Commissioner by Alderman Clare Winterbotham, Deputy Mayor.

ALFRED LORD TENNYSON (1809-92)
Poet Laureate
10 St. James's Square (map 1 no.1)

127 - Alfred Lord Tennyson

In 1844, shortly after the death of his father, poet Alfred Lord Tennyson was persuaded to invest the family fortune and earnings from his poetry, in woodcarving machinery. Unfortunately within months the venture had failed and he had lost most of his inheritance. The severe depression and hypochondria to which he was prone intensified to such a degree that it has been said that his life was feared for. At that time Tennyson's mother and sisters were renting a house at 10 St James's Square. He moved to Cheltenham to be with them and was prescribed rest, isolation and the Cheltenham waters in order to restore his health.

Tennyson avoided the fashionable side of town, describing it as '*a polka, parson-worshipping place of which Francis Close is Pope*', preferring the company of a few close friends, including the poet Sydney Dobell, the Rev. William Dobson, Cheltenham College principal 1844-9, and Frederick Robertson, Curate of Christ Church, who later became a celebrated preacher. Despite his disparaging remarks about Cheltenham, he used his mother's house in St James's Square as a base for six years, and it is thought that he wrote most of his epic poem *In Memoriam* there. When the poem was published in 1850 he succeeded Wordsworth as Poet Laureate.

The bronze plaque affixed to 10 St James's Square by the Public Libraries Committee records that Tennyson lived in the house from 1846-50. The plaque was unveiled by Sir James Agg-Gardner on 14 October 1926, and was probably the first commemorative plaque to be erected in the town.

128 - Unveiling the green plaque at the Electricity Sub-station, Clarence Street in 1986. Amongst the attendees was author Rev. W. Awdry, far right. See p.68.

129 - Cheltenham Civic Society commemorate the home of historian and print-maker George Rowe, whose Illustrated Cheltenham Guide is still widely consulted today. See p.44.

Map 1 - Jessop Avenue and West High Street

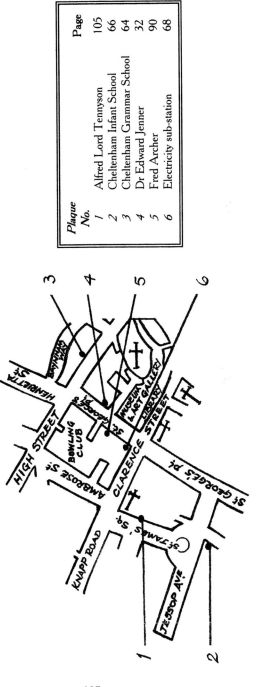

Plaque No.		Page
1	Alfred Lord Tennyson	105
2	Cheltenham Infant School	66
3	Cheltenham Grammar School	64
4	Dr Edward Jenner	32
5	Fred Archer	90
6	Electricity sub-station	68

Map 2 - East High Street and Cambray

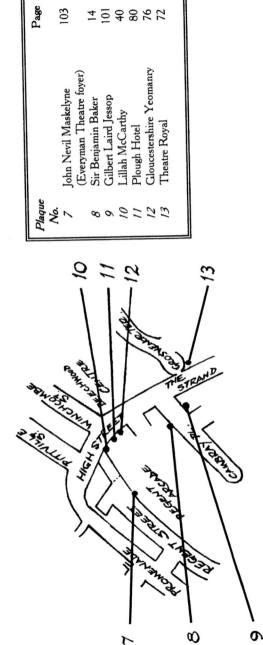

Map 3 - Pittville, Wellington Square and Clarence Square

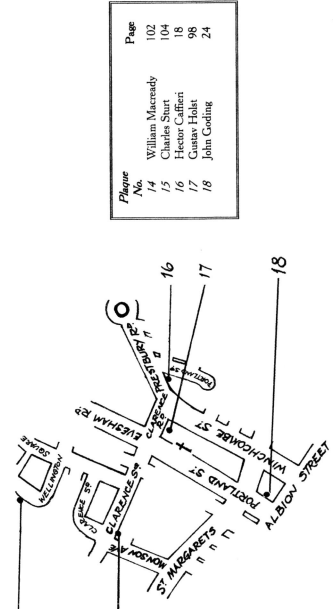

Plaque No.		Page
14	William Macready	102
15	Charles Sturt	104
16	Hector Caffieri	18
17	Gustav Holst	98
18	John Goding	24

Map 4 – London Road and Fairview

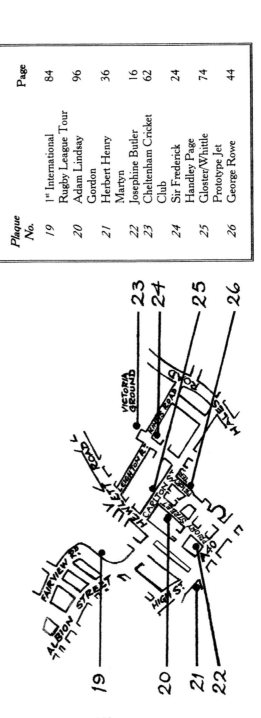

Map 5 - Montpellier and Bayshill

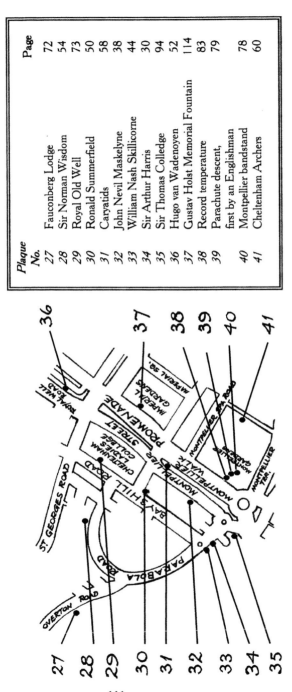

Map 6 - Lansdown

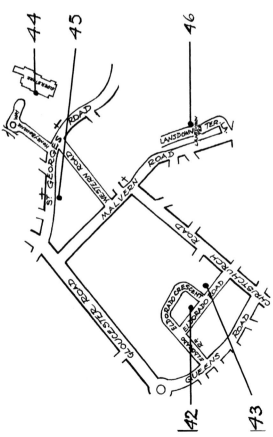

Map 7 - Suffolk Square and Tivoli

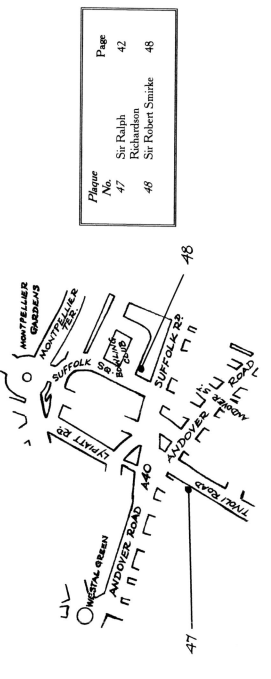

Plaque No.		Page
47	Sir Ralph Richardson	42
48	Sir Robert Smirke	48

Map 8 - Charlton Kings

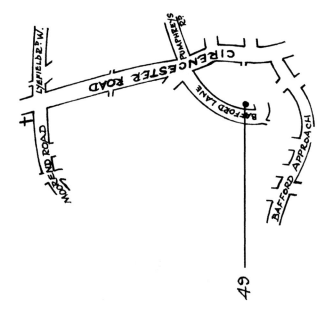

Plaque No.		Page
49	Cecil Day Lewis	20

CHRONOLOGICAL LIST OF PLAQUES

Listed in order of unveiling. Plaque number refers to the plaque's location on the maps on pp.107-14

Plaques marked ** were sponsored solely by the named individual or group.

All other plaques were co-sponsored by Cheltenham Civic Society

PAGE	PLAQUE NO.	COMMEMORATES	LOCATION	UNVEILED	SPONSORED BY	COMMENTS
105	1	ALFRED LORD TENNYSON (1809-92)	10 St James' Square	14 Oct 1926	Public Libraries Committee**	Poet Laureate
102	14	WILLIAM CHARLES MACREADY (1793-1873)	6 Wellington Square	15 Mar 1927	Public Libraries Committee**	Actor
96	20	ADAM LINDSAY GORDON (1833-70)	Court House, 28 Priory Street	19 Oct 1933	Douglas Brooke Wheelton Sladen**	'National poet of Australia'
103	7	JOHN NEVIL MASKELYNE (1839-1917)	Everyman Theatre, Regent Street	07 May 1947 06 Jun 2005	Cotswold Magical Society**	Illusionist & watchmaker. Originally on Old Town Hall. See also p.38.
104	15	CHARLES STURT (1795-1869)	19 Clarence Square	16 Jul 1948	Public Libraries Committee**	Explorer of Australia
100	45	DR EDWARD JENNER (1749-1823)	Alpha House, St George's Road	17 May 1949	Public Libraries Committee **	Pioneer of Vaccination. See also p.32

PAGE	PLAQUE NO.	COMMEMORATES	LOCATION	UNVEILED	SPONSORED BY	COMMENTS
98	17	GUSTAV HOLST (1874-1934)	4 Clarence Road	30 Jun 1949	Public Libraries Committee**	Composer
92	5	FRED ARCHER (1857-86)	St. George's Cottage, 43 St George's Place	Autumn 1971	Mrs M. Pratley **	Champion Jockey
101	9	GILBERT LAIRD JESSOP (1874-1955)	30 Cambray Place	04 Aug 1975	Gerald Brodribb**	Captain of Gloucestershire Cricket Club
94	35	SIR THOMAS RICHARDSON COLLEDGE (1796-1879)	Lauriston House, Montpellier Street	1976	Owners of Lauriston House**	Founder of Medical Missionary Society
28	24	SIR FREDERICK HANDLEY PAGE (1885-1962)	3 King's Road	22 Apr 1982	The Handley Page Association	Pioneering aircraft designer. First Civic Society plaque
18	34	SIR ARTHUR 'BOMBER' HARRIS (1892-1984)	Cranham Villa, 3 Queen's Parade	19 Sep 1982	R.A.F. Association, Cheltenham Branch	Wartime Commander of Bomber Command
42	47	SIR RALPH RICHARDSON (1902-83)	Charnes, 11 Tivoli Road	06 Nov 1982	National Theatre	Actor

PAGE	PLAQUE NO.	COMMEMORATES	LOCATION	UNVEILED	SPONSORED BY	COMMENTS
48	48	SIR ROBERT SMIRKE (1781-1867)	Montpellier House, Suffolk Square	30 Apr 1983	Gloucestershire Architectural Association	Architect
16	17	JOSEPHINE BUTLER (1828-1906)	Wellington Mansions, London Road	23 Jul 1983 16 Oct 1999	The Josephine Butler Association	Social reformer. (Originally on Mercian House, on same site. Demolished 1998)
20	49	CECIL DAY LEWIS (1904-72)	Box Cottage, Bafford Lane, Charlton Kings	08 Oct 1983	Cheltenham College	Poet Laureate
26	43	MARIE HALL (1884-1956)	Broadleas, 9 Eldorado Road	09 Jun 1984	Incorporated Society of Musicians	Violinist
44	26	GEORGE ROWE (1796-1864)	3 Priory Terrace	06 Oct 1984	British Printing Industries Federation. South Western District	Artist and print-maker
14	14	SIR BENJAMIN BAKER (1840-1907)	4 Cambray Place	19 Jan 1985	Institute of Civil Engineers	Civil engineer
40	10	LILLAH McCARTHY (1875-1960)	148 High Street	07 Sep 1985	Cheltenham Theatre and Arts Club	Actress

PAGE	PLAQUE NO.	COMMEMORATES	LOCATION	UNVEILED	SPONSORED BY	COMMENTS
18	16	HECTOR CAFFIERI (1847-1932)	21 Prestbury Road	15 Feb 1986	The Medici Society	Artist
68	6	ELECTRICITY. SUB-STATION	Corner of Clarence Street & St Georges Place	03 May 1986	Gloucestershire Society for Industrial Archaeology	Originally part of Borough's electricity network. Strozzi Palace apartment hotel from 2008
22	46	SIR GEORGE DOWTY (1901-75)	10 Lansdown Terrace Lane	04 Apr 1987	The Dowty Group	Aircraft engineer
66	2	CHELTENHAM INFANT SCHOOL	St James's Square	10 Oct 1987	College of St. Paul & St.Mary (now Univ. of Gloucestershire)	Oldest purpose-built infant school in existence
72	27	FAUCONBERG LODGE	Sidney Lodge, Overton Road	25 Jun 1988	Cheltenham Ladies' College	Bi-centenary of King George III's visit in 1788
72	13	THEATRE ROYAL	York Passage, Grosvenor Terrace	02 Jul 1988	Reeder & Richards	Bi-centenary of King George III's visit in 1788
73	29	ROYAL OLD WELL	Main entrance to Ladies' College, Bayshill Road	05 Jul 1988	Cheltenham Ladies' College	Bi-centenary of King George III's visit in 1788.
38	32	JOHN NEVIL MASKELYNE (1839-1917)	12 Rotunda Terrace, Montpellier	10 Jun 1989	Ogle Fine Arts	Illusionist and watchmaker. See also p. 103

PAGE	PLAQUE NO.	COMMEMORATES	LOCATION	UNVEILED	SPONSORED BY	COMMENTS
64	3	CHELTENHAM GRAMMAR SCHOOL	252-3 High Street	16 Mar 1993	Pates' Grammar School Foundation	Site of school founded by Richard Pate
78	40	MONTPELLIER BANDSTAND	Montpellier Gardens	20 Jul 1994	Friends of Montpellier Bandstand & Gardens	Originally red. Replaced with green plaque on 3 Oct 2008
74	25	ASSEMBLY GLOSTER WHITTLE E28/39 JET	Former Crabtree Garage, Carlton Street	25 Mar 1995	British Aerospace	Assembly of 2nd Jet prototype
32	4	DR. EDWARD JENNER (1749-1823)	22 St. George's Place	20 Apr 1995	Sovereign Housing Association	Pioneer of vaccination and 'father of immunology'. See also p. 100
24	24	JOHN GODING (1816-79)	3 Portland Street	14 Oct 1995	Cheltenham Local History Society	Historian of Cheltenham
80	11	PLOUGH HOTEL	Left of entrance to Regent Arcade	23 May 1997	Regent Arcade Shopping Centre	Cheltenham's leading hotel and coaching inn

PAGE	PLAQUE NO.	COMMEMORATES	LOCATION	UNVEILED	SPONSORED BY	COMMENTS
54	28	SIR NORMAN WISDOM (1915-)	Hotel du Vin, Parabola Road	06 Sep 2003	Carlton Hotel	Comedian Actor Singer
62	23	CHELTENHAM CRICKET CLUB	Pavilion, Victoria Cricket Ground	21 Jun 2004	Cheltenham Cricket Club	Pavilion opened by Dr W.G. Grace
82	38	RECORD TEMPERATURE (1990)	Montpellier Gardens	24 Jul 2004	Friends of Montpellier Bandstand and Gardens	Record temperature reading at Meteorological Station
36	21	H.H. MARTYN (1842-1937)	Stirling Court, London Road	02 Apr 2005	John Whittaker	Architectural art worker & philanthropist
84	19	CENTENARY FIRST INTERNATIONAL RUGBY LEAGUE TOUR (1908)	St. John's Avenue	15 Feb 2008	The Rugby League	England vs. New Zealand
60	40	CHELTENHAM ARCHERS (1857-2007)	Montpellier Gardens	26 Apr 2008	The Cheltenham Archers	Foundation of modern archery by Horace Ford
76	12	PARACHUTE DESCENT, FIRST BY ENGLISHMAN (1838)	Montpellier Gardens	03 Oct 2008	British Parachute Association	First successful descent, by John Hampton

PAGE	PLAQUE NO.	COMMEMORATES	LOCATION	UNVEILED	SPONSORED BY	COMMENTS
76	12	GLOUCESTERSHIRE YEOMANRY	Right of entrance to Regent Arcade	12 Sep 1997	Royal Gloucestershire Hussars	Gloucestershire Yeomanry first raised in 1795 at Plough Hotel
52	36	HUGO VAN WADENOYEN (1892-1959)	79 Promenade (part of Municipal Offices)	13 Jun 1998	Cheltenham Camera Club	Photographer
46	33	WILLIAM NASH SKILLICORNE (1807-87)	Royston, 9 Queen's Parade	12 Jun 1999	Cheltenham Borough Council	Cheltenham's first Mayor
50	30	RONALD SUMMERFIELD (1916-89)	Summerfield House, Bayshill Road	14 Apr 2000	The Summerfield Charitable Trust	Antiques collector & benefactor
58	44	CARYATIDS OF MONTPELLIER	1 Montpellier Walk	19 Jul 2002	Montpellier Traders' Association	Cheltenham's 'armless ladies'
86	43	ST JAMES'S STATION	Front entrance to Waitrose store, Honeybourne Way	02 Apr 2003	Gloucestershire Society for Industrial Archaeology	Cheltenham's Great Western Railway terminus
34	42	BRIAN JONES (1942-1969)	Rosemead, 17 Eldorado Road	03 Jul 2003	Brian Jones Fan Club	Founder member of the Rolling Stones

130 - The Gustav Holst Memorial Fountain in Imperial Gardens, designed by Anthony Stones FRBS, FRSA. Erected by the Civic Society in 2008, thanks to a generous legacy by Elizabeth Hamond, and with sponsorship from local companies. The Memorial is located on the site of the old Imperial Gardens bandstand. See map 5 no.37.